Weight Watchers™

Slim & Trim '96

The Weight Watchers Programme Cookbook   Wendy Veale

SIMON & SCHUSTER
A VIACOM COMPANY

First published in Great Britain by Simon & Schuster, 1996
A Viacom Company

Simon & Schuster Ltd
West Garden Place
Kendal Street
London W2 2AQ

Design: Green Moore Lowenhoff
Typesetting: Stylize
Photography: Iain Bagwell
Styling: Rachel Jukes
Food preparation: Jane Stevenson

Weight Watchers Publications Manager: Delia Bintley
Weight Watchers Publications Assistant: Celia Whiston

A CIP catalogue record is available from the British Library

ISBN 0-671-51246-3

Printed and bound in Italy by Rotolito Lombarda S.p.A.

Pictured on the front cover: *Braised Lamb Chops (page 53) and Hot Chicken Salad (page 33)*

Pictured on the back cover: *Golden Vegetable Bake and Tuna and Pasta Bake (page 41)*

Recipe notes:
Egg size is medium (size 3), unless otherwise stated.
Vegetables are medium-size, unless otherwise stated.
It is important to use proper measuring spoons, not cutlery, for spoon measures.
1 tablespoon = 15 ml; 1 teaspoon = 5 ml.
Dried herbs can be substituted for fresh ones, but the flavour may not always
be as good. Halve the fresh-herb quantity stated in the recipe.

Vegetarian recipes:
These symbols show which recipes are suitable for vegetarians.

V shows the recipe is vegetarian

V shows the recipe has a vegetarian option

The Slim and Trim Programme for men and young people:
The recipes in this book have been designed to fit the Slim and Trim '96 daily
Selection totals for women. The Selections remaining per day are those for women.
On the Slim and Trim Programme men and young people aged between 10 and
16 should eat additional Carbohydrate, Fruit, Milk and Protein Selections. Full
details can be found within the Programme Material. For further information
call 01628 777077.

Contents

Introduction

How often have you been told that you should eat three proper meals a day? For some people it may sound like just too much trouble. For others, especially those who are trying to lose weight, three meals a day may simply sound like too much food. After all, you didn't join the world's most successful slimming organisation to learn how to overeat! However, if you have been with Weight Watchers for any time at all, or if you're a Lifetime Member like me, you'll know that following the Slim and Trim Programme – which means eating three square meals a day – is the most successful and healthy way to lose weight, and to keep it off. Weight Watchers Slim and Trim Programme will not leave you hungry, lessening your resolve to lose weight. Instead it will satisfy you with tasty and filling food, including puddings and treats to spur you on. This cookbook has been designed around the Slim and Trim Programme. The recipes are such that you can enjoy three proper meals each day – simply choose any Breakfast, Light Meal and Main Meal. All of the recipes give Selections per serving and, best of all, they fit the Slim and Trim '96 guidelines (see Programme Material for details). In most cases you won't be using the full range of Selections available, so you can afford to treat yourself – perhaps by trying one of the Dessert recipes. You'll also find that some of the Light and Main Meal recipes don't make use of the Fruit Selection. Women may have one with each meal, or else save it for a snack. Some recipes include Optional Calories – if you are following the Slim and Trim Programme you must remember to count these on a weekly basis. To make your planning even easier, each recipe indicates the Daily Selections that you will have left after that meal. ≈≈ Weight Watchers is sure you'll find this cookbook a big help on your way to a slimmer and trimmer you. And best of all, you'll quickly discover – like millions of Members before you – that losing weight doesn't have to mean losing out!

Breakfasts

Breakfast is perhaps the easiest meal to skip. Time is so often of the essence – the kids need a kick-start, the dog needs to be walked – there are always so many 'needs' to be met and it will be you who loses out if you don't take a few moments for yourself. So start the day as you mean to go on – with a nourishing and delicious breakfast. After all, by morning your body has been without food for quite a stretch and it needs nutrients and Calories to wake it up and prepare it for the day ahead.

Breakfast in a Bap

Serves 1

Preparation and cooking time:
10 minutes
Calories per serving: 170

Freezing not recommended

Start the day as you mean to go on! Tasty and satisfying, this breakfast bap is made in minutes and can be eaten on the run.

2 open mushrooms, sliced
2 teaspoons low-fat spread
$\frac{1}{2}$ oz (15 g) lean back bacon rasher
1 tomato, halved
1 oz (30 g) bap, halved
2 teaspoons brown sauce
salt and freshly ground black pepper

1. Preheat the grill to hot. Place the mushrooms on a piece of foil. Dot with the low-fat spread. Lay the bacon rasher on top and the tomato halves alongside. Grill for 5–8 minutes (turning the bacon over after a few minutes) until the bacon is crispy.
2. Place the bap on the edge of the grill pan for a few minutes to lightly toast or warm it through.
3. Spread the brown sauce over one half of the bap and place the mushrooms, bacon and tomato on top. Season with salt and freshly ground black pepper, and then sandwich the bap together and serve at once.

Selections per serving:
1 Carbohydrate; 1 Fat; 1 Protein; 1 Vegetable; 10 Optional Calories

Selections remaining per day:
3–5 Carbohydrate; 1–2 Fat; 2–3 Fruit; 2 Milk; 2–5 Protein; 2 Vegetable

Baked Egg and Mushrooms

Serves 1

Preparation and cooking time:
15 minutes
Calories per serving: 230

Freezing not recommended

(V) If using a free-range egg

This is a breakfast to take your time over – perfect with freshly brewed coffee and the morning paper!

2 button mushrooms
1 teaspoon margarine
$\frac{1}{2}$ teaspoon chopped fresh chives or parsley
1 egg
1 tablespoon single cream
1 oz (30 g) slice of brown bread
1 teaspoon sun-dried or regular tomato paste
salt and freshly ground black pepper
a pinch of paprika, to serve

1. Bring a small saucepan of water (one-third full) to the boil. Blanch the mushrooms for 2 minutes, and then remove them with a slotted spoon and pat them dry with kitchen paper, reserving the boiled water. Halve and roughly chop the mushrooms.
2. Grease a small ramekin dish or teacup with the margarine. Place the mushrooms and chives or parsley in the base, and then carefully crack in the egg. Season with salt and freshly ground black pepper. Spoon the cream over the surface.
3. Drop a small metal pastry cutter into the saucepan – this will act as a trivet. Cover the ramekin dish or teacup with a piece of foil and carefully place on the trivet. Cover the saucepan.
4. Steam the egg for 6–8 minutes, or until cooked to your liking.
5. Meanwhile, toast the slice of bread and spread it with the tomato paste. Cut in fingers.
6. Sprinkle a little paprika over the egg and serve with the toast.

Selections per serving:
1 Carbohydrate; 1 Fat; 1 Protein; 50 Optional Calories

Selections remaining per day:
3–5 Carbohydrate; 1–2 Fat; 2–3 Fruit; 2 Milk; 2–5 Protein; 3 Vegetable

Granola

Makes 10 × 1¹/₂ oz (45 g) servings

Preparation and cooking time:	5 oz (150 g) porridge oats
30 minutes	4 oz (120 g) wheatflakes or
Calories per serving: 160	branflakes
	1 oz (30 g) wheatgerm
Freezing not recommended	5 teaspoons sunflower seeds
	5 teaspoons desiccated coconut
Ⓥ	4 fl oz (120 ml) unsweetened
	apple juice
This delicious and nutritious	2 teaspoons clear honey
breakfast cereal is similar to	2 oz (60 g) sultanas
crumbly flapjack. Serve it	1 oz (30 g) dried apricots,
with skimmed milk or low-fat	chopped
natural yogurt from your daily	1 oz (30 g) dried apples,
allowance.	chopped

1. Preheat the oven to Gas Mark 4/180°C/350°F. Mix together the oats, wheatflakes or branflakes, wheatgerm, sunflower seeds and coconut in a large bowl. Stir in the apple juice and honey.
2. Spread the mixture on to 2 non-stick baking trays. Bake for 20 minutes, stirring occasionally so that the cereal browns evenly.
3. Let the mixture cool and stir in the dried fruit. Transfer to an airtight container.
4. Weigh out 1¹/₂ oz (45 g) per single portion and serve with skimmed milk or low-fat natural yogurt from your daily allowance.

Selections per serving:
1 Carbohydrate; 45 Optional Calories

Selections remaining per day:
3–5 Carbohdyrate; 2–3 Fat; 2–3 Fruit; 2 Milk; 3–6 Protein; 3 Vegetable

Variation:
You may have 1 Fruit Selection with your granola but remember to deduct it from your Selections remaining per day.

For 1 Fruit Selection choose from 1 medium-size chopped pear or 1 small sliced banana.

For ¹/₂ Fruit Selection choose from 1 oz (30 g) chopped ready-to-eat prunes, 2 oz (60 g) seedless grapes, or 2 oz (60 g) fresh raspberries.

Porridge with Cinnamon and Apricots

Serves 1

Preparation and cooking time:	1 oz (30 g) porridge oats
10 minutes	¹/₄ pint (150 ml) skimmed milk
Calories per serving: 275	2 oz (60 g) ready-to-eat dried
	apricots, chopped
Freezing not recommended	¹/₄ teaspoon ground cinnamon
	1 teaspoon brown sugar
Ⓥ	a pinch of salt

This hearty porridge will provide a warming start to any cold winter's day.

1. Place the porridge oats in a small saucepan. Add the milk and a pinch of salt. Bring to the boil, and then lower the heat and simmer for 5–6 minutes, stirring occasionally.
2. Mix together the chopped apricots, cinnamon and brown sugar. Pour the porridge into a warm bowl and sprinkle with the apricot topping. Serve at once.

Selections per serving:
1 Carbohydrate; 1 Fruit; ¹/₂ Milk; 20 Optional Calories

Selections remaining per day:
3–5 Carbohydrate; 2–3 Fat; 1–2 Fruit; 1¹/₂ Milk; 3–6 Protein; 3 Vegetable

Variation:
Replace the dried apricots with 1 small sliced banana or 1 oz (30 g) chopped sultanas.

Cheesy Scotch Pancakes

Serves 2

Preparation and cooking time:	2 eggs, separated
25 minutes	2 oz (60 g) plain flour
Calories per serving: 360	a drop of artificial sweetener
	4 oz (120 g) cottage cheese
Freezing not recommended	3 tablespoons skimmed milk
	a pinch of ground cinnamon
Ⓥ If using free-range eggs	1/4 teaspoon cream of tartar
	2 teaspoons vegetable oil
No need to wait until Shrove	a pinch of salt
Tuesday – these little pancakes	**To serve:**
are delicious at any time with	2 small bananas, sliced
fresh fruit, jam or just on their	1/2 lemon, cut in wedges
own with a squeeze of lemon.	

1. Blend the egg yolks, flour, artifical sweetener, cottage cheese, milk, cinnamon and a pinch of salt in a liquidiser or food processor for 20 seconds, or until smooth.
2. Whisk together the egg whites and cream of tartar in a grease-free bowl until stiff. Fold the egg whites into the pancake batter.
3. Heat a small, heavy-based frying pan. Add a few drops of oil and pour in just enough batter to make a pancake approximately 4 inches (10 cm) in diameter. When it begins to brown on the edges and small air bubbles appear on the exposed surface, turn it over with a spatula and cook the other side. Make 6 pancakes in total, keeping them warm.
4. Serve at once with the sliced banana and lemon wedges.

Cook's note:
These pancakes are best eaten fresh, but can be individually wrapped in clingfilm and kept for a day or two in the refrigerator. Warm them up in the oven or under the grill.

Selections per serving:
1 Carbohydrate; 1 Fat; 1 Fruit; 1 Protein; 65 Optional Calories

Selections remaining per day:
3–5 Carbohydrate; 1–2 Fat; 1–2 Fruit; 2 Milk; 2–5 Protein; 3 Vegetable

Variation:
These pancakes are delicious with low-fat natural yogurt. Spoon on 5 tablespoons and deduct 1/2 Milk Selection from your Selections remaining per day.

Cheese and Tomato Crumpets

Serves 2

Preparation and cooking time:	2 × 1 oz (30 g) crumpets
10 minutes	4 teaspoons low-fat spread
Calories per serving: 230	1 teaspoon Marmite
	2 small tomatoes, sliced
Freezing not recommended	2 oz (60 g) Cheddar cheese, grated
Ⓥ If using vegetarian cheese	freshly ground black pepper

1. Preheat the grill to hot. Lightly toast the crumpets on both sides, and then spread with the low-fat spread and the Marmite.
2. Top each crumpet with a sliced tomato, season with freshly ground black pepper and sprinkle with the Cheddar cheese. Grill for 4–5 minutes until the cheese is bubbling. Serve at once.

Cook's note:
Keep a bag of grated cheese in your freezer. It is quick and convenient, and saves on washing up first thing in the morning.

Selections per serving:
1 Carbohydrate; 1 Fat; 1 Protein; 1 Vegetable; 5 Optional Calories

Selections remaining per day:
3–5 Carbohdyrate; 1–2 Fat; 2–3 Fruit; 2 Milk; 2–5 Protein; 2 Vegetable

Dried Fruit Compote

Makes 8 × 2 oz (60 g) servings

Preparation time:
10 minutes + 12 hours soaking
Calories per serving: 230

Freezing not recommended

(V)

This fragrant spiced fruit compote is delicious eaten warm or chilled. It will keep for up to a week in the refrigerator during which time its flavours really develop.

8 oz (240 g) mixed dried fruits (e.g., prunes, apricots, figs and apples)
thinly peeled zest of ½ medium-size orange
2-inch (5 cm) piece of cinnamon stick
4 cardamom pods, crushed lightly
4 cloves
4 teaspoons honey
1 pint (600 ml) strong hot tea
artificial sweetener, to taste
To serve:
1 oz (30 g) muesli, per serving
5 tablespoons low-fat natural yogurt, per serving

1. Place the fruits in a large bowl. Stir in the orange zest, cinnamon stick, cardamom and cloves.
2. Drizzle the honey over and pour in the hot tea. Cover with clingfilm and leave to stand until cold.
3. Refrigerate for 12 hours or overnight to allow the fruits to soften and the flavours to develop. Adjust the sweetness, as desired, with a few drops of artificial sweetener.
4. Serve warm or cold, accompanied with 1 oz (30 g) of muesli and 5 tablespoons of low-fat natural yogurt.

Cook's note:
As a short cut, at step 2 the compote can be brought to the boil and then simmered gently in a saucepan for approximately 15 minutes. This eliminates the time required for soaking the fruits.

Selections per serving:
1 Carbohydrate; 1 Fruit; 1½ Milk; 10 Optional Calories

Selections remaining per day:
3–5 Carbohydrate; 2–3 Fat; 1–2 Fruit; ½ Milk; 3–6 Protein; 3 Vegetable

Variations:
Omit the muesli and enjoy the compote on its own as a mid–morning snack or dessert.
    Substitute 1 oz (30 g) slice of wholewheat toast for the muesli.

Light Meals

As the Slim and Trim Programme fits around your own routine, Light Meals can be eaten at lunchtime or in the evening, whenever you prefer. And whatever your needs or mood, you will find a tasty recipe to suit. Some of the recipes are ideal for packed lunches – Smoked Fish Pâté (page 26) or Pineapple and Prawn Pitta Pockets (page 20) – while others are perfect to come home to on a rainy day. There's nothing like a bowl of warming soup to fill in the gap until dinner, and with recipes like Cauliflower Cheese Soup (page 17) you'll look forward to winter afternoons!

Fresh Pear with Creamy Blue Cheese

Serves 1

Preparation time: 10 minutes
Calories per serving: 385

Freezing not recommended

V If using vegetarian cheese

The contrast in flavour between the sharp tangy cheese and smooth sweet pear is so good that this will no doubt become a favourite Light Meal.

1 very ripe medium-size pear, sliced
2 teaspoons lemon juice
1 oz (30 g) strong blue cheese (e.g., Gorgonzola or Stilton)
2 tablespoons natural fromage frais (up to 8% fat)
½ oz (15 g) chopped walnuts
freshly ground black pepper
fresh watercress, to garnish
To serve:
cherry tomatoes
1 oz (30 g) slice brown bread

1. Brush the pear slices with the lemon juice and fan out on a dessert plate.
2. Cream together the blue cheese and fromage frais. Stir in the walnuts and season with ground black pepper. Spoon over the pears.
3. Garnish with fresh watercress and serve with the cherry tomatoes and fresh brown bread.

Selections per serving:
1 Carbohydrate; 1 Fat; 1 Fruit; 2 Protein; 1 Vegetable

Selections per day remaining:
3–5 Carbohydrate; 1–2 Fat; 1–2 Fruit; 2 Milk; 1–4 Protein; 3 Vegetable

Cracked Wheat Salad

Serves 2

Preparation time: 40 minutes + 30 minutes chilling
Calories per serving: 265

Freezing not recommended

Known in the Mediterranean as *tabbouleh*, this filling and nourishing salad is delicious served on its own or with ham, cooked prawns or cold chicken.

2 oz (60 g) bulgar wheat
2 tomatoes, skinned and diced
4-inch (10 cm) piece of cucumber, diced
2 spring onions, sliced thinly
1 small garlic clove, chopped
3 tablespoons lemon juice
2 teaspoons olive oil
2 teaspoons chopped fresh parsley
2 teaspoons chopped fresh mint
salt and freshly ground black pepper
To serve:
mixed green salad leaves
4 oz (120 g) ham, sliced thinly

1. Place the bulgar wheat in a bowl, cover it with boiling water and leave it to soak for 30 minutes. Drain and then wrap it in a clean tea towel. Squeeze hard to remove any excess moisture.
2. Return the drained bulgar wheat to the bowl and stir in the rest of the ingredients, except for the salad leaves and ham. Season well, and then cover and chill for 30 minutes. Serve on a bed of salad leaves with 2 oz (60 g) sliced ham per portion.

Selections per serving:
1 Carbohydrate; 1 Fat; 2 Protein; 2 Vegetable

Selections remaining per day:
3–5 Carbohydrate; 1–2 Fat; 2–3 Fruit; 2 Milk; 1–4 Protein; 1 Vegetable

V Vegetarian Option:
Omit the ham and serve with 2 oz (60 g) of vegetarian feta cheese per serving, crumbled over the top.

Cauliflower Cheese Soup

Serves 2

Preparation time: 10 minutes
Cooking time: 25 minutes
Calories per serving: 340

Freezing recommended
(at the end of step 2)

Ⓥ If using vegetarian cheese

Cauliflower cheese is such a popular dish – so why not enjoy the same delicious combination in a soup!

1 small or ¹/₂ medium-size
  cauliflower, chopped roughly
1 shallot or small onion,
  quartered
¹/₄ pint (150 ml) skimmed milk
1 tablespoon cornflour
2 oz (60 g) mature Cheddar
  cheese, grated
salt and freshly ground black
  pepper
1 teaspoon fresh snipped
  chives, to garnish
To serve:
2 × 2 oz (60 g) brown bread
  rolls
4 teaspoons low-fat spread

1. Cook the cauliflower and shallot or onion in lightly salted boiling water for 15–20 minutes or until tender. Drain, reserving ¹/₄ pint (150 ml) of the cooking water. Purée the cauliflower and shallot or onion with the reserved cooking water in a liquidiser or food processor until smooth. Return to the saucepan.
2. Blend the milk with the cornflour and stir into the soup. Bring to the boil, stirring constantly until the soup thickens. Reduce the heat and simmer for 10 minutes. Season to taste.
3. Stir in all but 2 teaspoons of the grated cheese. Ladle into 2 warm bowls and sprinkle with the remaining cheese and snipped chives. Serve at once with the rolls, spread with the low-fat spread.

Cook's note:
Use Gruyère cheese or a blue cheese for a change of taste.

Selections per serving:
2 Carbohydrate; 1 Fat; ¹/₄ Milk; 1 Protein; 1 Vegetable;
15 Optional Calories

Selections remaining per day:
2–4 Carbohydrate; 1–2 Fat; 2–3 Fruit; 1³/₄ Milk; 2–5 Protein;
2 Vegetable

Variation:
Replace 1 oz (30 g) of the cheese with ¹/₂ oz (15 g) lean back bacon, grilled until crispy and crumbled on to the soup before serving.

Mushroom Soup

Serves 2

Preparation and cooking time:
30 minutes
Calories per serving: 280

Freezing recommended
(for the soup only)

Ⓥ

A warming soup is so welcoming on a chilly winter's day. This makes a filling and satisfying Light Meal.

4 teaspoons low-fat spread
1 small onion, chopped finely
4 oz (120 g) open mushrooms,
  sliced
¹/₄ pint (150 ml) vegetable stock
¹/₄ pint (150 ml) skimmed milk
¹/₂ tablespoon chopped fresh
  thyme or ¹/₂ teaspoon dried
  thyme
1 teaspoon cornflour
1 tablespoon sherry
2 oz (60 g) thick-sliced white
  bread
4 oz (120 g) low-fat soft cheese
1 garlic clove, chopped finely
1 teaspoon chopped fresh
  parsley
salt and freshly ground black
  pepper

1. Melt the low-fat spread in a medium-size saucepan. Cook the onion gently for 5 minutes until well softened. Add the mushrooms and cook for 5 minutes more.
2. Stir in the stock, milk and thyme. Bring to the boil and then cover, reduce the heat and simmer for 15 minutes.
3. Transfer the soup to a liquidiser or food processor and blend for 20 seconds until smooth. Return the soup to a clean saucepan. Blend the cornflour and sherry together and stir into the soup. Reheat, stirring gently until the soup thickens slightly. Season with salt and pepper and simmer for 5 minutes more.
4. Meanwhile, toast the sliced bread under a hot grill. Mix together the soft cheese, garlic and parsley, and season with salt and pepper. Spread over one side of the toast. Cut the toast in cubes and pop them back under the grill for 2 minutes or until the cheese has melted slightly.
5. Ladle the soup into warm bowls. Scatter with the croûtons and serve at once.

Selections per serving:
1 Carbohydrate; 1 Fat; ¹/₄ Milk; 1 Protein; 1 Vegetable;
15 Optional Calories

Selections remaining per day:
3–5 Carbohydrate; 1–2 Fat; 2–3 Fruit; 1³/₄ Milk; 2–5 Protein;
2 Vegetable

Prawn and Tomato Soup

Serves 2

Preparation and cooking time:
30 minutes
Calories per serving: 230

Freezing not recommended

Enjoy this delicious soup either hot or well chilled.

2 teaspoons olive oil
1 small onion, chopped
1 garlic clove, crushed
7 oz (210 g) canned chopped
  tomatoes
6 oz (180 g) canned pimentos,
  drained and chopped
2 teaspoons tomato purée
1/2 pint (300 ml) fish or
  vegetable stock
4 oz (120 g) cooked peeled
  prawns
2 teaspoons cornflour
1 tablespoon chopped fresh
  parsley
2 oz (60 g) thick-sliced white
  bread, cubed
salt and freshly ground black
  pepper

1. Heat the oil in a large saucepan. Gently cook the onion and garlic for 5 minutes until softened. Add the chopped tomatoes and pimentos. Reduce the heat and simmer for 5 minutes.
2. Add the tomato purée, stock and prawns. Cover and simmer for 10 minutes more.
3. Transfer the soup to a liquidiser or food processor and blend for about 20 seconds or until smooth. Return to the saucepan and reheat very gently until almost boiling. Preheat the grill.
4. Blend the cornflour with a little cold water. Stir it into the soup and continue stirring until the soup thickens slightly. Season with salt and freshly ground black pepper. Stir in the chopped parsley and simmer for 5 minutes more.
5. Toast the bread cubes under the grill, turning them frequently. Serve the soup in warm bowls and sprinkle with the croûtons, dividing them equally between the 2 bowls.

Cook's notes:
If you prefer, you can omit the pimentos and substitute an extra 7 oz (210 g) canned chopped tomatoes.
   On hot days, you can serve the soup chilled, replacing the croûtons with a 1 oz (30 g) bread roll per serving.

Selections per serving:
1 Carbohydrate; 1 Fat; 1 Protein; 2½ Vegetable;
10 Optional Calories

Selections remaining per day:
3–5 Carbohydrate; 1–2 Fat; 2–3 Fruit; 2 Milk; 2–5 Protein;
½ Vegetable

Jambalaya

Serves 2

Preparation and cooking time:
30 minutes
Calories per serving: 420

Freezing recommended

This spicy rice dish originates in Mississippi. Similar to paella, it is easy to make and will certainly liven up your taste buds!

2 teaspoons vegetable oil
1 small onion, sliced
1 garlic clove, chopped
1 oz (30 g) mushrooms, sliced
1 small green pepper, diced
3 oz (90 g) long-grain rice
1/4 pint (150 ml) beef or chicken
  stock
7 oz (210 g) canned chopped
  tomatoes
1 tablespoon tomato purée
1/2 teaspoon chilli powder
1/2 teaspoon ground allspice
1/2 teaspoon dried oregano
1/2 teaspoon dried thyme
2 oz (60 g) chorizo sausage
  or salami, sliced
4 oz (120 g) cooked peeled
  prawns
1 tablespoon chopped fresh
  parsley
salt

1. Heat the oil in a saucepan and gently cook the onion and garlic for 5 minutes until softened. Stir in the mushrooms, green pepper and rice and cook for 2 minutes more. Add the stock and chopped tomatoes and bring to the boil.
2. Stir in the tomato purée, chilli powder, allspice, oregano, thyme and sliced chorizo or salami. Reduce the heat, cover and simmer for 15 minutes or until the rice has absorbed the stock and is tender.
3. Stir in the prawns and chopped parsley and season with salt. Serve on warm plates.

Cook's note:
Chorizo is a Spanish spicy sausage made with pork, cayenne pepper and spices. Most delicatessens and supermarkets stock it. You can, however, substitute cooked ham or salami if you prefer.

Selections per serving:
1 Carbohydrate; 1 Fat; 2 Protein; 1 Vegetable; 40 Optional Calories

Selections per day remaining:
3–5 Carbohydrate; 1–2 Fat; 2–3 Fruit; 2 Milk; 1–4 Protein;
2 Vegetable

Melon with Prawns

Serves 2

Preparation and cooking time:
15 minutes
Calories per serving: 305

Freezing not recommended

**Sweet juicy chunks of melon
with prawns in a cool dressing
makes a perfect Light Meal for
a summer picnic.**

8 oz (240 g) honeydew melon,
  cubed
6 tablespoons natural fromage
  frais (up to 8%) fat
2 tablespoons single cream
1 tablespoon lime juice
1 teaspoon clear honey
1 tablespoon chopped fresh
  coriander
4 oz (120 g) cooked peeled
  prawns
assorted salad leaves
salt and freshly ground black
  pepper
fresh coriander leaves, to
  garnish

To serve:
2 × 1 oz (30 g) slices brown
  bread
4 teaspoons low-fat spread

1. Place the melon cubes in bowl. In another bowl, beat together
the fromage frais, single cream, lime juice and honey. Season with
salt and pepper and stir in the chopped coriander.
2. Fold the dressing in with the melon cubes. Cover and refrigerate
for 10 minutes, and then fold in the prawns.
3. Arrange some salad leaves on 2 individual serving plates. Spoon
the melon and prawn mixture evenly over the salad leaves. Garnish
with fresh coriander leaves and serve at once with the bread and
low-fat spread.

Cook's note:
Keep an eye out for the fresh lime juice now available in small
squeezy bottles.

Selections per serving:
1 Carbohydrate; 1 Fat; 1 Fruit; 1 Protein; 1 Vegetable;
105 Optional Calories

Selections remaining per day:
3–5 Carbohydrate; 1–2 Fat; 1–2 Fruit; 2 Milk; 2–5 Protein;
2 Vegetable

Variations:
Replace the prawns with 2 oz (60 g) cooked diced chicken.
Alternatively, serve the melon and creamy dressing with 2 oz (60 g)
smoked salmon slices or smoked trout fillets.
    Substitute chopped fresh dill, tarragon or mint for the coriander.

Pineapple and Prawn Pitta Pockets

Serves 1

Preparation and cooking time:
10 minutes
Calories per serving: 325

Freezing not recommended

**Use either 2 mini or 1 large
pitta bread to stuff with this
delicately curried prawn and
salad filling.**

2 oz (60 g) canned pineapple in
  natural juice, drained and
  chopped
1 oz (30 g) Chinese leaf, endive
  or white cabbage, shredded
2 oz (60 g) cooked peeled
  prawns
1 small tomato, chopped
1-inch (2.5 cm) piece of
  cucumber, diced
1 tablespoon low-fat natural
  yogurt
2 teaspoons low-calorie
  mayonnaise
2 teaspoons mango chutney
1/2 teaspoon mild curry paste
  or powder
2 oz (60 g) pitta bread
salt and freshly ground black
  pepper

1. Mix together the pineapple, shredded Chinese leaf, endive or
white cabbage, prawns, tomato and cucumber in a bowl. Season
well with salt and pepper.
2. In a separate bowl, mix together the yogurt, mayonnaise, mango
chutney and curry paste or powder until smooth. Fold this in with
the salad mixture.
3. Warm the pitta bread and split open. Spoon in the salad and
serve at once.

Cook's note:
Try to use curry paste rather than the powder. It has a better flavour
and will blend more easily into the dressing.

Selections per serving:
2 Carbohydrate; 1 Fat; 1 Protein; 1 Vegetable; 80 Optional Calories

Selections remaining per day:
2–4 Carbohydrate; 1–2 Fat; 2–3 Fruit; 2 Milk; 2–5 Protein;
2 Vegetable

V Vegetarian Option:
Omit the prawns and substitute 1 tablespoon of peanut butter
for the curry paste. The Selections and Optional Calories will
remain the same.

Italian Open Sandwich

Serves 1

Preparation time: 10 minutes
Calories per serving: 310

Freezing not recommended

'Pronto' to prepare – and with endless variations, enjoy the flavours of the Mediterranean in this tasty open sandwich.

2 teaspoons tomato purée
2 × ¹/₂ oz (15 g) slices of French bread, cut on the diagonal
assorted lettuce leaves (e.g., frisée, Little Gem, lollo rosso)
1 oz (30 g) sliced salami
1 shallot, sliced
1 tomato, diced
1 teaspoon olive oil
1 teaspoon grated parmesan cheese
salt and freshly ground black pepper
torn basil leaves, to garnish

1. Spread the tomato purée over each slice of bread. Divide and arrange the salad leaves, salami, sliced shallot and diced tomato on top of each slice.
2. Drizzle the olive oil over. Season with salt and freshly ground black pepper. Sprinkle with the parmesan cheese, garnish with the torn basil leaves and serve at once.

Cook's note:
Keep an eye out for the Italian breads now available. Ciabatta bread can be used instead of French bread.

Selections per serving:
1 Carbohydrate; 1 Fat; 1 Protein; 1 Vegetable; 10 Optional Calories

Selections remaining per day:
3–5 Carbohydrate; 1–2 Fat; 2–3 Fruit; 2 Milk; 2–5 Protein; 2 Vegetable

Variation:
Arrange 2 small sliced black olives on the open sandwich, adding 10 Optional Calories.

V Vegetarian option:
Replace the salami with a sliced hard-boiled egg.

Toasted Ham and Apricot Muffin

Serves 1

Preparation and cooking time: 10 minutes
Calories per serving: 350

Freezing not recommended

This yummy muffin is ideal for a quick and warm Light Meal and makes a perfect tea-time treat for all the family.

1 oz (30 g) muffin, split
2 teaspoons low-fat spread
2 oz (60 g) low-fat soft cheese
2 oz (60 g) canned apricot halves in natural juice, drained and sliced with 2 tablespoons of the juice reserved
¹/₂ teaspoon snipped fresh chives
¹/₄ green pepper, de-seeded and diced
1 oz (30 g) ham, sliced thinly and cut in strips
salt and freshly ground black pepper

1. Preheat the grill to medium. Lightly toast the muffin halves on both sides and top with the low-fat spread.
2. Cream the soft cheese with the reserved juice from the canned apricots. Season with salt and pepper and divide half of the cheese spread between the two muffin halves.
3. Scatter the snipped chives and green pepper over the muffins.
4. Place half of the apricot slices on the muffins and cover with strips of ham. Arrange the remaining apricot slices on top and coat with the rest of the cheese spread.
5. Grill for 4–5 minutes until the cheese is lightly set and golden brown. Serve at once.

Cook's note:
Keep an eye out for the wafer-thin American-style ham. You appear to get a lot more for the weight!

Selections per serving:
1 Carbohydrate; 1 Fat; 2 Protein; 30 Optional Calories

Selections remaining per day:
3–5 Carbohydrate; 1–2 Fat; 2–3 Fruit; 2 Milk; 1–4 Protein; 3 Vegetable

Variation:
Use pineapple in natural juice instead of apricot, topping the ham with a pineapple ring.

Warm Smoked Haddock Salad

Serves 1

Preparation and cooking time:
25 minutes
Calories per serving: 230

Freezing not recommended

This delicious warm salad
incorporates an innovative
way of cooking fish. It works
just as well with smoked
salmon, but is not quite
so economical!

4 oz (120 g) small new potatoes
4 oz (120 g) fresh smoked
  haddock

1 teaspoon olive oil
1 teaspoon lemon juice
assorted salad leaves
freshly ground black pepper
To garnish:
fresh dill sprigs
lemon wedge
For the dressing:
1-inch (2 cm) piece of
  cucumber, diced
2 tablespoons low-fat natural
  yogurt
2 teaspoons lemon juice
2 teaspoons chopped fresh dill
salt and freshly ground black
  pepper

1. Make the dressing by placing all the ingredients in a screw-topped jar and shaking well to combine. Season with salt and pepper and chill until required.
2. Meanwhile, cook the potatoes in lightly salted boiling water for 15 minutes, or until tender. Drain and keep warm.
3. Preheat the grill. Slice the haddock in paper-thin slivers and arrange in one layer on a large flameproof dish. Mix the olive oil and lemon juice together and brush it over the fish. Season with freshly ground black pepper. Place under the grill for 3–4 minutes or until the fish becomes opaque.
4. Arrange some salad leaves in the centre of the plate. Spoon the potatoes on and drizzle the dressing over the top.
5. Garnish with fresh dill and a lemon wedge and serve at once.

Cook's note:
Pop the smoked haddock into the freezer for half an hour to make it easier to slice thinly.

Selections per serving:
1 Carbohydrate; 1 Fat; 2 Protein; 1 Vegetable; 20 Optional Calories

Selections remaining per day:
3–5 Carbohydrate; 1–2 Fat; 2–3 Fruit; 2 Milk; 1–4 Protein;
2 Vegetable

Kedgeree

Serves 2

Preparation and cooking time:
40 minutes
Calories per serving: 405

Freezing not recommended

Originating in British
India and generally served
at breakfast, kedgeree is
a delicious Light Meal
and can be eaten hot or cold.

4 oz (120 g) wholegrain brown
  rice
1 large onion, chopped
4 oz (120 g) smoked haddock
  fillet

2 oz (60 g) cooked peeled
  prawns
2 tablespoons chopped fresh
  parsley
1/2–1 teaspoon curry paste
  or powder
2 teaspoons olive oil
juice of 1/2 lemon
2 tablespoons low-fat natural
  yogurt
1 egg, hard-boiled and
  quartered, to garnish
4 oz (120 g) green beans,
  to serve

1. Cook the rice according to pack instructions. Ten minutes before the end of its cooking time, stir in the onion and continue cooking until the rice is tender. Drain and keep warm.
2. Meanwhile, place the fish and 4 tablespoons of water into a small saucepan. Bring to the boil, and then immediately remove the pan from the heat, cover with a lid and leave for 10 minutes. The fish will continue to cook, becoming opaque and flaking easily.
3. Drain the fish liquor into a measuring jug. Skin and flake the fish, discarding any bones. Fold the fish into the hot cooked rice along with the prawns and parsley.
4. Whisk the curry paste or powder, olive oil, lemon juice and yogurt into the reserved fish liquor. Pour the sauce over the rice and lightly mix everything together.
5. Divide the kedgeree between 2 warm plates and garnish with the hard-boiled egg. Serve warm or cold with lightly boiled green beans.

Selections per serving:
2 Carbohydrate; 1 Fat; 2 Protein; 1 Vegetable; 15 Optional Calories

Selections remaining per day:
2–4 Carbohydrate; 1–2 Fat; 2–3 Fruit; 2 Milk; 1–4 Protein;
2 Vegetable

Variation:
Replace the cooked smoked haddock with 4 oz (120 g) canned tuna fish or 2 oz (60 g) fresh smoked salmon.

Smoked Fish Pâté with Crudités

Serves 4

Preparation time: 10 minutes
+ 30 minutes chilling
Calories per serving: 300

**Freezing recommended
(for up to 4 weeks)**

Quick and easy to prepare,
these individual pâtés are
great for packed lunches and
for lunchtime entertaining.

4 oz (120 g) smoked fish fillets
 (i.e., trout or mackerel)
2 shallots or 1 small onion
1 oz (30 g) white bread, cubed
2 oz (60 g) low-fat soft cheese
4 teaspoons mayonnaise
2 tablespoons low-fat natural
 yogurt
1 tablespoon lemon juice
1 teaspoon horseradish relish
a pinch of paprika
salt and freshly ground black
 pepper
lemon slices, to garnish
To serve:
4 × 1 oz (30 g) pitta bread
12 oz (360 g) assorted vegetable
 crudités (e.g., sticks of celery,
 carrot and red pepper, whole
 radishes and cherry
 tomatoes)

1. Remove any skin or bones from the fish. Place in a food
processor or liquidiser with the shallots or onion and bread cubes.
Process until chopped very finely.
2. Add the soft cheese, mayonnaise, yogurt, lemon juice and
horseradish and process again until the mixture is soft and smooth.
Season with a pinch of paprika and salt and freshly ground black
pepper to taste. Add a little more lemon juice, if desired.
3. Divide the pâté between 4 individual ramekin dishes. Cover
and chill for at least 30 minutes.
4. Garnish each dish with a twist of lemon and serve with fresh
pitta bread and a selection of crisp vegetable crudités.

Cook's note:
If you enjoy a packed lunch, freeze a quantity of individual pâtés.
Remove one from the freezer first thing in the morning and by
lunchtime it will have thawed out.

Selections per serving:
1 Carbohydrate; 1 Fat; 1 Protein; 1 Vegetable; 40 Optional Calories

Selections remaining per day:
3–5 Carbohydrate; 1–2 Fat; 2–3 Fruit; 2 Milk; 2–5 Protein;
2 Vegetable

Mexican Salad with Tortilla Chips

Serves 2

Preparation time: 10 minutes
+ 15 minutes chilling
Calories per serving: 365

Freezing not recommended

Ⓥ If using vegetarian cheese

2 spring onions, chopped finely
½ small red pepper, de-seeded
 and chopped finely
2 tomatoes, chopped finely
1 fresh red or green chilli,
 de-seeded and chopped finely
1 small garlic clove, chopped
 finely
2 teaspoons olive oil
juice of 1 lime
1 tablespoon fresh chopped
 coriander
1 teaspoon caster sugar
salt and freshly ground black
 pepper
To serve:
2 oz (60 g) tortilla chips
4 oz (120 g) melon, sliced
2 oz (60 g) Cheddar cheese,
 grated

1. Mix together all the ingredients except the tortilla chips,
melon and cheese. Adjust the seasoning to taste, cover and chill
for 15 minutes.
2. Divide the tortilla chips and the melon between 2 plates; spoon
on the spring onion, tomato and pepper mixture. Scatter with the
grated cheese. Serve at once.

Cook's note:
Do not touch your eyes or mouth when handling chillies. Wash
your hands thoroughly afterwards.

Selections per serving:
1 Carbohydrate; 1 Fat; 1 Protein; 1 Vegetable;
120 Optional Calories

Selections remaining per day:
3–5 Carbohydrate; 1–2 Fat; 2–3 Fruit; 2 Milk; 2–5 Protein;
2 Vegetable

Variation:
Try using 2 oz (60 g) of crumbled Feta cheese instead of
the Cheddar.

Curried Egg with Rice

Serves 1

Preparation and cooking time:
30 minutes
Calories per serving: 355

Freezing not recommended

Ⓥ If using a free-range egg

This Bombay-style egg is simply delicious! The mild and creamy curried sauce perfectly complements the flavour of eggs.

1 teaspoon vegetable oil
1 shallot or a small onion, chopped finely
1 teaspoon mild curry powder
1 teaspoon flour
¼ pint (150 ml) vegetable stock
1½ oz (45 g) long-grain rice
1 egg, hard-boiled
2 tablespoons low-fat natural yogurt
salt and freshly ground black pepper
To garnish:
a pinch of paprika
fresh coriander sprigs
To serve:
1 tomato, sliced
½ spring onion, sliced

1. Heat the oil in a saucepan and gently cook the shallot or onion for 3–4 minutes until softened. Sprinkle in the curry powder and flour and cook, stirring, for 2 minutes more.
2. Gradually blend in the stock, stirring constantly until the sauce comes to the boil and thickens. Reduce the heat, cover and simmer for 10 minutes.
3. Meanwhile, cook the rice in lightly salted boiling water for 10–12 minutes. Drain and spoon on to a warm serving plate.
4. Shell and halve the egg and place, yolk side down on top of the rice. Stir the yogurt into the sauce, season with salt and pepper and spoon over the eggs. Garnish with a dusting of paprika and fresh coriander sprigs. Serve at once with the tomato and spring onion.

Cook's note:
Try serving this hot with a poached egg instead of a hard-boiled egg.

Selections per serving:
1 Carbohydrate; 1 Fat; 1 Protein; 1 Vegetable; 70 Optional Calories

Selections remaining per day:
3–5 Carbohydrate; 1–2 Fat; 2–3 Fruit; 2 Milk; 2–5 Protein; 2 Vegetable

Cheese and Onion Puffed Omelette

Serves 1

Preparation and cooking time:
15 minutes
Calories per serving: 350

Freezing not recommended

Ⓥ If using free-range eggs and vegetarian cheese

This is an impressive, yet easy way of making an omelette light and fluffy.

1 teaspoon olive oil
2 spring onions or 1 shallot, chopped finely
2 eggs, separated
¼ teaspoon dried tarragon
2 teaspoons grated parmesan cheese
salt and freshly ground black pepper
To serve:
4 oz (120 g) boiled new potatoes
3 oz (90 g) steamed courgettes

1. Heat the oil in a small non-stick omelette pan. Sauté the spring onions or shallot for 3–4 minutes, or until softened. Transfer to a bowl using a slotted spoon.
2. Add the egg yolks, tarragon and 1 teaspoon of the parmesan cheese. Beat well and season with salt and freshly ground black pepper.
3. Place the egg whites in a grease-free bowl and whisk until stiff. Carefully fold them into the yolk mixture.
4. Pre-heat the grill to hot. Pour the mixture into the hot omelette pan and cook gently for 4–5 minutes until lightly set.
5. Sprinkle the remaining parmesan cheese over the surface of the omelette and pop it under the hot grill until golden brown. Serve at once, accompanied by the new potatoes and steamed courgettes.

Selections per serving:
1 Carbohydrate; 1 Fat; 2 Protein; 1 Vegetable; 20 Optional Calories

Selections remaining per day:
3–5 Carbohydrate; 1–2 Fat; 2–3 Fruit; 2 Milk; 1–4 Protein; 2 Vegetable

Variation:
Add 1 small chopped tomato or 2 sliced button mushrooms at step 1.

Stuffed Mushrooms

Serves 2

Preparation and cooking time:
15 minutes
Calories per serving: 300

Freezing not recommended

Ⓥ *If using vegetarian cheese*

These large stuffed mushrooms are full of flavour and go well with a tomato and onion salad.

4 large mushrooms (open flat variety)
2 teaspoons olive oil
1 shallot or small onion, chopped finely
1 garlic clove, chopped finely
2 oz (60 g) fresh wholemeal breadcrumbs
4 oz (120 g) cottage cheese with chives
1 egg, beaten
1/2 oz (15 g) parmesan cheese, grated finely
4 tablespoons skimmed milk
salt and freshly ground black pepper
chopped fresh parsley, to garnish
For the salad:
4 medium-size tomatoes, sliced
1 red onion, sliced thinly
2 teaspoons chopped fresh basil
2 teaspoons white wine vinegar

1. Preheat the oven to Gas Mark 6/200°C/400°F. Remove the stalks from the mushrooms and chop finely.
2. Heat the oil in a frying pan and cook the shallot or onion and garlic until softened. Add the mushroom stalks and cook for 2 minutes more.
3. Remove the saucepan from the heat and stir in the breadcrumbs, cottage cheese and beaten egg. Mix thoroughly and season with salt and freshly ground black pepper.
4. Divide the stuffing evenly between the mushroom caps and sprinkle with the parmesan cheese. Place on a shallow baking tray. Pour a drop of milk around each mushroom to prevent them from drying out. Cook for 20 minutes.
5. Meanwhile, arrange the sliced tomatoes on two individual side plates. Scatter the onion rings and chopped basil on top. Drizzle with the vinegar and season with salt and pepper.
6. Serve the mushrooms hot, garnished with fresh chopped parsley and accompanied by the tomato and onion salad.

Selections per serving:
1 Carbohydrate; 1 Fat; 1 Protein; 1 Vegetable; 55 Optional Calories

Selections remaining per day:
3–5 Carbohydrate; 1–2 Fat; 2–3 Fruit; 2 Milk; 2–5 Protein; 2 Vegetable

Savoury Mushroom Omelette

Serves 1

Preparation and cooking time:
15 minutes
Calories per serving: 385

Freezing not recommended

Ⓥ *If using a free-range egg and vegetarian cheese*

2 teaspoons low-fat spread
1 shallot or small onion, chopped finely
1 small garlic clove, chopped finely
4 oz (120 g) button mushrooms, sliced thinly
1 egg, beaten
3 tablespoons skimmed milk
1 oz (30 g) mature Cheddar cheese, grated
salt and freshly ground black pepper
chopped fresh parsley, to garnish
1 oz (30 g) bread roll, to serve

1. Melt the low-fat spread in a 7-inch (18 cm) non-stick frying pan. Add the shallot or onion and garlic and cook gently for 5 minutes, until softened. Add the mushrooms and continue to cook for 5 minutes, stirring occasionally.
2. Beat together the egg and milk. Season with salt and freshly ground black pepper and pour over the mushrooms. Cook gently for 4 minutes more.
3. Preheat the grill to high. Sprinkle the cheese over the omelette and cook for 1 minute. Place under the hot grill until the surface is golden and bubbling. Slide the omelette on to a warm plate, garnish with the chopped parsley and serve at once with a bread roll.

Selections per serving:
1 Carbohydrate; 1 Fat; 2 Protein; 1 Vegetable; 15 Optional Calories

Selections remaining per day:
3–5 Carbohydrate; 1–2 Fat; 2–3 Fruit; 2 Milk; 1–4 Protein; 2 Vegetable

Variation:
Replace half the Cheddar cheese with 1/2 oz (15 g) ham or salami, chopped finely and added in with the mushrooms. This will make it unsuitable for vegetarians.

Fruity Ham and Celery Salad

Serves 2

Preparation time: 15 minutes
+ chilling
Calories per serving: 305

Freezing not recommended

2 oz (60 g) thick slice of lean
  ham, cut in strips
2 celery sticks, chopped
2 oz (60 g) cooked long-grain
  rice
4 oz (120 g) canned pineapple
  pieces in natural juice,
  drained
1/2 small red or yellow pepper,
  de-seeded and diced

4 tablespoons low-fat natural
  yogurt
4 teaspoons low-calorie
  mayonnaise
1 teaspoon Dijon mustard
2 teaspoons chopped fresh
  herbs (e.g., chives and
  parsley)
1 medium-size dessert apple,
  sliced
2 teaspoons lemon juice
1 Little Gem lettuce
salt and freshly ground black
  pepper
2 × 1 oz (30 g) bread rolls,
  to serve

1. Fold together the ham, celery, cooked rice, pineapple pieces
and pepper.
2. Meanwhile, make the dressing. Mix the yogurt, mayonnaise,
mustard and fresh chopped herbs in a small bowl. Season well
with salt and pepper. Fold the dressing into the ham mixture.
Cover and chill.
3. Brush the apple slices with the lemon juice. Divide the lettuce
between 2 serving plates. Spoon on the ham salad and garnish with
the apple slices. Serve at once with the bread rolls.

Selections per serving:
1 Carbohydrate; 1 Fat; 1 Fruit; 1 Protein; 1 Vegetable;
45 Optional Calories

Selections remaining per day:
3–5 Carbohydrate; 1–2 Fat; 1–2 Fruit; 2 Milk; 2–5 Protein;
2 Vegetable

Variation:
Replace the ham with 2 oz (60 g) of sliced cooked sausage or spicy
chorizo sausage.

V Vegetarian option:
Replace the ham with 2 chopped hard-boiled eggs.

Hot Chicken Salad

Serves 1

Preparation and cooking time:
15 minutes
Calories per serving: 240

Freezing not recommended

**Smoked chicken tastes even
more delicious than plain
chicken in this big salad. Keep
your eye out for it in the
supermarket.**

1 teaspoon olive oil
1 teaspoon wine vinegar
1/2 teaspoon Dijon mustard
1 teaspoon chopped fresh
  chives

1 teaspoon chopped fresh
  tarragon
a pinch of dried garlic granules
3 oz (90 g) skinless, boneless
  chicken breast
1 oz (30 g) button mushrooms,
  sliced
4 cherry tomatoes, halved
2 spring onions, trimmed and
  sliced
assorted salad leaves (e.g.,
  spinach, lollo rosso, Iceberg),
  shredded
salt and freshly ground black
  pepper
1 oz (30 g) French bread,
  to serve

1. Preheat the grill to medium-high.
2. Mix together the olive oil, wine vinegar, mustard, chives,
tarragon and garlic granules in a screw-topped jar. Season with salt
and pepper and give it a good shake. Chill until required.
3. Meanwhile, grill the chicken breast on a raised rack for 3–4
minutes on either side, until the chicken is tender and cooked
through.
4. Arrange the mushrooms, tomatoes and spring onions on a bed
of salad leaves. Cut the chicken in strips and arrange on top.
Drizzle the chilled dressing over the salad and serve at once with
the French bread.

Selections per serving:
1 Carbohydrate; 1 Fat; 2 Protein; 1 Vegetable

Selections remaining per day:
3–5 Carbohydrate; 1–2 Fat; 2–3 Fruit; 2 Milk; 1–4 Protein;
2 Vegetable

Variations:
Substitute duck breast or salmon for the chicken.
    Instead of having French bread with your salad, add 3 oz (90 g)
of sweetcorn kernels.

Pasta Amatriciana

Serves 1

Preparation and cooking time:
30 minutes
Calories per serving: 430

Freezing recommended
(for the sauce only)

Named after a town in Italy,
this fiery sauce is quick to
make, and delicious when
tossed in with your favourite
pasta.

1 teaspoon vegetable oil
1 oz (30 g) salami, cut in strips
1 shallot or small onion, sliced
    finely
7 oz (210 g) canned chopped
    tomatoes
¹⁄₄ teaspoon dried crushed
    chillies
artificial sweetener, to taste
2 oz (60 g) pasta shapes
1 tablespoon chopped fresh
    parsley (optional)
salt and freshly ground black
    pepper

1. Heat the oil in a small saucepan and gently sauté the salami
and shallot or onion for 4–5 minutes. Add the canned tomatoes
and crushed chillies, bring to the boil and then simmer, uncovered,
for 5 minutes.
2. Add a drop of artificial sweetener, and season to taste with salt
and freshly ground black pepper. Cover and simmer for 10 minutes
more.
3. Meanwhile, cook the pasta in plenty of lightly salted boiling
water for 8–10 minutes or until just *'al dente'*. Drain.
4. Fold the pasta and chopped parsley into the sauce and pour
it into a warm bowl. Serve at once.

Cook's note:
Keep an eye out for the handy 1 oz (30 g) packs of salami now
available at supermarket delicatessen counters. These are ideal
for solo cooking.

Selections per serving:
2 Carbohydrate; 1 Fat; 1 Protein; 2 Vegetable

Selections remaining per day:
2–4 Carbohydrate; 1–2 Fat; 2–3 Fruit; 2 Milk; 2–5 Protein;
1 Vegetable

Mushroom Pasta Toss

Serves 1

Preparation and cooking time:
15 minutes
Calories per serving: 385

Freezing not recommended

(V) **If using vegetarian cheese**

There are so many ways of
enjoying pasta when following
the Weight Watchers
Programme. Here's a quick-
and-easy pasta recipe with
mushrooms.

2 oz (60 g) tagliatelle, fettucini
    or spaghetti
1 teaspoon olive oil
4 oz (120 g) mushrooms, wiped
    and sliced
2 spring onions, chopped finely
1 garlic clove, chopped finely
2 tablespoons white wine or dry
    sherry
2 oz (60 g) low-fat soft cheese
1 tablespoon chopped fresh
    parsley
salt and freshly ground black
    pepper

1. Cook the pasta in plenty of lightly salted boiling water for
8–10 minutes or until *'al dente'*.
2. Meanwhile, heat the oil in a medium-size saucepan. Gently
sauté the mushrooms, spring onions and garlic for 4–5 minutes.
Sprinkle in the wine or sherry, and then cover and turn off the
heat, leaving the saucepan on the hob while you get ready to add
the remaining ingredients.
3. Drain the cooked pasta. Fold into the mushrooms along with
the soft cheese and chopped parsley. Season with salt and pepper
to taste. Pour into a warm bowl and serve at once.

Cook's note:
Use open, dark-gilled mushrooms in this recipe for their strong
flavour.

Selections per serving:
2 Carbohydrate; 1 Fat; 1 Protein; 1 Vegetable; 25 Optional Calories

Selections remaining per day:
2–4 Carbohydrate; 1–2 Fat; 2–3 Fruit; 2 Milk; 2–5 Protein;
2 Vegetable

Leek and Potato Salad with Crispy Bacon

Serves 1

Preparation and cooking time:
25 minutes
Calories per serving: 190

Freezing not recommended

Crispy hot bacon makes a delicious contrast to this cold leek and potato salad.

4 oz (120 g) new potatoes, scrubbed but not peeled
1 small leek, washed and trimmed
2 tablespoons low-fat natural yogurt
1 teaspoon olive oil
2 teaspoons white wine or cider vinegar
1 teaspoon clear honey
1 teaspoon horseradish relish or coarse-grained mustard
½ teaspoon mustard seeds
½ teaspoon fresh snipped chives
½ oz (15 g) lean back bacon rasher
salt and freshly ground black pepper

1. Boil the potatoes in lightly salted boiling water for 10 minutes. Add the whole leek and cook for 5 minutes more, or until the potatoes are tender and the leek is very lightly cooked. Drain the vegetables and refresh them under cold running water. Drain again.
2. Meanwhile, make the dressing. Mix together the yogurt, oil, vinegar, honey, horseradish or mustard, mustard seeds and chives in a bowl. Season with salt and pepper to taste.
3. Slice the leek and potato and carefully fold them into the dressing. Transfer to a serving plate, cover and chill for 10 minutes.
4. Meanwhile, cook the bacon under a very hot grill until it is crispy. Allow it to cool slightly. Crumble the bacon over the leek and potato salad and serve at once.

Selections per serving:
1 Carbohydrate; 1 Fat; 1 Protein; ½ Vegetable; 50 Optional Calories

Selections remaining per day:
3–5 Carbohydrate; 1–2 Fat; 2–3 Fruit; 2 Milk; 2–5 Protein; 2½ Vegetable

Stuffed Jacket Potato with Cottage Cheese and Mexican Salsa

Serves 2

Preparation time: 15 minutes
Cooking time: 1 hour
Calories per serving: 235

Freezing not recommended

Ⓥ

Liven up some cottage cheese with chillies and tomatoes to make a great filling for potatoes!

1 × 8 oz (240 g) potato
4 oz (120 g) cottage cheese
1 ripe tomato, de-seeded and diced
1 small fresh green chilli, de-seeded and diced
1-inch (2.5 cm) piece of cucumber, diced
juice of 1 lime
1 tablespoon single cream
1 teaspoon chopped fresh oregano
2 teaspoons margarine
salt and freshly ground black pepper
a pinch of paprika, to garnish
6 oz (180 g) steamed broccoli, to serve

1. Preheat the oven to Gas Mark 6/200°C/400°F. Prick the potato with a fork and bake for about 1 hour, or until tender.
2. Meanwhile, mix together the cottage cheese, diced tomato, chilli, cucumber, lime juice, cream and oregano. Season with salt and freshly ground black pepper.
3. Halve the baked potato, scoop out the insides into a bowl and reserve the skins. Mash the cooked potato with the margarine and fold in the cottage cheese filling.
4. Pack the filling back into the potato skins. Sprinkle with the paprika and serve half a potato per person, accompanied by the steamed broccoli.

Selections per serving:
1 Carbohydrate; 1 Fat; 1 Protein; 1 Vegetable; 25 Optional Calories

Selections remaining per day:
3–5 Carbohydrate; 1–2 Fat; 2–3 Fruit; 2 Milk; 2–5 Protein; 2 Vegetable

Stuffed Jacket Potato with Creamy Hummus

Serves 2

Preparation time: 15 minutes
Cooking time: 1 hour 10 minutes
Calories per serving: 250

Freezing not recommended

Ⓥ

Hummus is renowned for its high fat content. Here is a compromise on the original, delicious in this jacket potato.

1 × 8 oz (240 g) potato
2 teaspoons olive oil
1 shallot or small onion, chopped finely
1 garlic clove, chopped finely
1/4 teaspoon ground coriander
1/4 teaspoon ground cumin
6 oz (180 g) canned chick peas, drained
4 tablespoons low-fat natural yogurt
2 tablespoons chopped fresh coriander
salt and freshly ground black pepper
mixed green salad, to serve

1. Preheat the oven to Gas Mark 6/200°C/400°F. Prick the potato with a fork and bake for about 1 hour or until tender. Halve the potato, scoop the insides into a bowl, mashing them lightly, and reserve the skins.
2. Meanwhile, heat the oil in a small pan and gently cook the shallot or onion and garlic for 5 minutes, or until softened. Add the ground coriander and cumin and cook for 1 minute more.
3. Remove from the heat. Stir in the chick peas, yogurt and coriander, and add the mashed potato. Mix together well, seasoning with salt and pepper to taste.
4. Pack the potato skins with the creamy hummus mixture and return them to the oven for 10–15 minutes to heat through. Serve hot, half a potato per person, accompanied by a mixed green salad.

Cook's note:
The potato can be microwaved on 'HIGH' for 5 minutes and then finished off in the oven once it has been filled.

Selections per serving:
1 Carbohydrate; 1 Fat; 1 Protein; 1 Vegetable; 20 Optional Calories

Selections remaining per day:
3–5 Carbohydrate; 1–2 Fat; 2–3 Fruit; 2 Milk; 2–5 Protein; 2 Vegetable

Stuffed Jacket Potato with Apple, Celery and Grapes

Serves 2

Preparation time: 10 minutes
Cooking time: 1 hour
Calories per serving: 330

Freezing not recommended

Ⓥ

Similar in taste to a Waldorf salad, this filling is crisp and fruity.

1 × 8 oz (240 g) potato
1/2 medium-size red-skinned dessert apple, chopped
2 teaspoons lemon juice
1 small celery stick, chopped
1/2 oz (15 g) red seedless grapes, quartered
4 teaspoons low-calorie mayonnaise
1/2 oz (15 g) walnuts, chopped
3 oz (90 g) low-fat soft cheese
salt and freshly ground black pepper
fresh snipped chives, to garnish
8 oz (240 g) boiled mange-tout or green beans, to serve

1. Preheat the oven to Gas Mark 6/200°C/400°F. Prick the potato with a fork and bake for about 1 hour or until tender.
2. Meanwhile, toss the chopped apple in the lemon juice, and then mix in the celery, grapes, mayonnaise and walnuts (reserving a few for garnish). Season with salt and freshly ground black pepper.
3. Halve the baked potato, scoop out the insides and reserve the skins. Mix the low-fat soft cheese in with the potato. Season with salt and freshly ground black pepper and pack back into the skins.
4. Divide the apple and celery mixture and pile it on top of the potato halves, sprinkling on the few reserved chopped walnuts. Top with the snipped chives and serve at once, accompanied by freshly cooked mange-tout or green beans.

Selections per serving:
1 Carbohydrate; 1 Fat; 1 Protein; 1 1/2 Vegetable; 35 Optional Calories

Selections remaining per day:
3–5 Carbohydrate; 1–2 Fat; 2–3 Fruit; 2 Milk; 2–5 Protein; 1 1/2 Vegetable

Variation:
Replace the apple and grapes with 1 medium-size orange, segmented and chopped. Your Optional Calories will become 25.

Tuna and Pasta Bake

Serves 1

Preparation time: 10 minutes
Cooking time: 25 minutes
Calories per serving: 320

Freezing not recommended

2 oz (60 g) canned tuna in
  brine, drained
2 oz (60 g) cottage cheese
1 teaspoon olive oil
1 small courgette, sliced
½ teaspoon dried mixed herbs
3 oz (90 g) cooked pasta shells
7 oz (210 g) canned chopped
  tomatoes
½ oz (15 g) mature Cheddar
  cheese, grated finely
salt and freshly ground black
  pepper

1. Preheat the oven to Gas Mark 5/190°C/375°F.
2. Gently mix together the tuna and cottage cheese. Lightly grease a small ovenproof dish with the olive oil. Line the bottom with half of the sliced courgette, and then spoon on half of the tuna and cottage cheese mixture, a pinch of herbs and half of the cooked pasta. Season with salt and freshly ground black pepper.
3. Repeat the layers, ending with the pasta. Pour the canned chopped tomatoes over, and then sprinkle with the grated cheese.
4. Cook for 20–25 minutes until bubbling and golden brown.

Cook's note:
3 oz (90 g) cooked pasta is equivalent to 1 oz (30 g) uncooked pasta which equals 1 Carbohydrate Selection.

Selections per serving:
1 Carbohydrate; 1 Fat; 2 Protein; 3 Vegetable; 30 Optional Calories

Selections remaining per day:
3–5 Carbohydrate; 1–2 Fat; 2–3 Fruit; 2 Milk; 1–4 Protein

V Vegetarian option:
Replace the tuna fish with either 3 oz (90 g) canned red kidney beans or 2 oz (60 g) diced Quorn.

Golden Vegetable Bake

Serves 1

Preparation time: 30 minutes
Cooking time: 15 minutes
Calories per serving: 385

Freezing recommended

V If using vegetarian cheese

This creamy gratin of winter root vegetables with its crispy topping is simply delicious!

2 teaspoons low-fat spread
1 shallot or small onion, diced
2 oz (60 g) carrots, sliced thinly
4 oz (120 g) parsnips, sliced
  thinly
2 oz (60 g) swede, diced
½ teaspoon ground cumin
1 tablespoon crème fraîche
  or single cream
1 teaspoon chopped fresh
  parsley
1 oz (30 g) fresh wholemeal
  breadcrumbs
1 oz (30 g) mature Cheddar
  cheese, grated finely
salt and freshly ground black
  pepper
a sprig of fresh parsley, to
  garnish

1. Melt the low-fat spread in a saucepan. Gently cook the shallot or onion for 3–4 minutes until softened. Add the carrots, parsnips and swede plus 2 tablespoons of water. Season with salt and pepper. Cover and simmer gently for 20 minutes, shaking the saucepan occasionally.
2. Preheat the oven to Gas Mark 5/190°C/375°F. Drain the cooked vegetables and purée them in a food processor or blender together with the ground cumin, crème fraîche or cream, and parsley. Season with salt and pepper.
3. Spoon the purée into an individual ovenproof gratin dish. Mix together the breadcrumbs and cheese and spread them over the purée. Bake for 15 minutes until the top is crisp and golden brown. Serve at once, garnished with the fresh parsley.

Selections per serving:
2 Carbohydrate; 1 Fat; 1 Protein; 1 Vegetable; 50 Optional Calories

Selections remaining per day:
2–4 Carbohydrate; 1–2 Fat; 2–3 Fruit; 2 Milk; 2–5 Protein; 2 Vegetable

Variation:
Substitute potato for the parsnip.

Salmon with Tomato and Cucumber Dressing

Serves 1

Preparation and cooking time:
20 minutes
Calories per serving: 315

Freezing not recommended

4 oz (120 g) new potatoes
1 teaspoon olive oil
3 oz (90 g) salmon fillet
   or steak
2 tablespoons white wine

1 teaspoon lemon juice
1 tomato, peeled, de-seeded
   and diced
1-inch (2.5 cm) piece of
   cucumber, peeled, de-seeded
   and diced
1 teaspoon snipped fresh chives
salt and freshly ground black
   pepper
assorted salad leaves, to serve

1. Cook the potatoes in lightly salted boiling water for 10–15 minutes, or until just tender.
2. Meanwhile, heat the oil in a small non-stick frying pan and sauté the salmon over a high heat for 2–3 minutes on each side. Remove and wrap in foil to keep warm.
3. Add the wine, lemon juice, tomato, cucumber and chives to the pan and bring rapidly to the boil. Immediately remove from the heat and season with salt and pepper.
4. Drain the potatoes and arrange them with the cooked salmon and assorted salad leaves on a warm serving plate. Spoon the hot cucumber and tomato dressing over the salmon and drizzle the juices over the salad leaves. Serve at once.

Selections per serving:
1 Carbohydrate; 1 Fat; 2 Protein; 1 Vegetable; 25 Optional Calories

Selections remaining per day:
3–5 Carbohydrate; 1–2 Fat; 2–3 Fruit; 2 Milk; 1–4 Protein; 2 Vegetable

Main Meals

Main Meals may sound like hard work, but these recipes will prove the opposite. Quick and easy to prepare, without compromising on taste, these meals will both appeal to adventurous tastebuds and satisfy the traditionalist in us all.

Bacon Filled Vegetables

Serves 1

Preparation time: 20 minutes
Cooking time: 20 minutes
Calories per serving: 485

Freezing not recommended

vegetables of your choice, for stuffing (e.g., 1 small red pepper, halved and de-seeded; 1 large courgette, halved and de-seeded; 2 large flat mushrooms, stalks removed and chopped; or 1 small aubergine, halved and de-seeded)
1 teaspoon grated parmesan cheese
salt and freshly ground black pepper
1 oz (30 g) crusty roll, to serve

For the filling:
1 teaspoon olive oil
1 oz (30 g) lean back bacon rasher, chopped with rind removed
1 spring onion, chopped very finely
1 garlic clove, crushed (optional)
2 button mushrooms, chopped finely
1 tomato, chopped finely
3 oz (90 g) cooked long-grain rice
1/2 teaspoon chopped fresh parsley
a dash of tabasco sauce
1 tablespoon tomato ketchup
1 oz (30 g) mozzarella cheese, grated
salt and freshly ground black pepper

1. Preheat the oven to Gas Mark 5/190°C/375°F. To make the filling, heat the oil in a saucepan and sauté the bacon, spring onion, garlic (if using) and mushrooms for 5 minutes, until softened.
2. Add the tomato and cook for 2 minutes more, and then stir in the remaining ingredients and season to taste.
3. Place the prepared vegetables hollow sides up in a baking dish and pack them with the filling. Cover with foil and bake for 15 minutes. Remove the foil, sprinkle the parmesan cheese over the stuffing and cook for 5 minutes more. Serve hot with the bread roll.

Selections per serving:
2 Carbohydrate; 1 Fat; 3 Protein; 3 Vegetable; 25 Optional Calories

Selections remaining per day:
2–4 Carbohydrate; 1–2 Fat; 2–3 Fruit; 2 Milk; 0–3 Protein

Leek and Ham Rolls with Parsley Sauce

Serves 2

Preparation and cooking time: 25 minutes
Calories per serving: 405

Freezing not recommended

2 large leeks, trimmed and halved
8 oz (240 g) new potatoes
2 teaspoons margarine
1 1/2 oz (45 g) plain flour
1/2 pint (300 ml) skimmed milk
2 tablespoons fresh chopped parsley
4 × 1 oz (30 g) slices of lean ham
1/2 oz (15 g) fresh breadcrumbs
2 teaspoons grated parmesan cheese
salt and freshly ground black pepper

1. Cook the leeks in lightly salted boiling water for 10 minutes. Drain, reserving 1/4 pint (150 ml) of the cooking water.
2. Cook the potatoes in lightly salted boiling water for 15 minutes, or until cooked through. Drain and keep warm.
3. Meanwhile, make the parsley sauce. Place the margarine, flour and milk in a saucepan. Heat gently, stirring constantly with a wire whisk until the mixture boils and thickens.
4. Whisk the reserved cooking water into the sauce together with the chopped parsley. Season with salt and pepper.
5. Preheat the grill to medium. Wrap the ham slices around the leeks. Lay them, seam-side down, in a shallow ovenproof dish. Pour the sauce over. Mix the breadcrumbs and cheese together and sprinkle them over the top.
6. Grill for 3–4 minutes or until the crumbs are golden brown and the sauce is bubbling. Serve at once with the new potatoes.

Selections per serving:
2 Carbohydrate; 1 Fat; 1/2 Milk; 2 Protein; 1 Vegetable; 10 Optional Calories

Selections remaining per day:
2–4 Carbohydrate; 1–2 Fat; 2–3 Fruit; 1 1/2 Milk; 1–4 Protein; 2 Vegetable

Honey Glazed Turkey

Serves 1

Preparation time: 10 minutes
+ 2 hours marinating
Cooking time: 10 minutes
Calories per serving: 340

Freezing not recommended

3 oz (90 g) skinless, boneless
   turkey breast
1 shallot or small onion,
   chopped finely
1 garlic clove, chopped finely

2 teaspoons clear honey
1 teaspoon vegetable oil
grated zest of ½ lime
juice of 1 lime
¼ teaspoon ground ginger
¼ teaspoon dried oregano
salt and freshly ground black
   pepper
8 oz (240 g) new potatoes,
   halved
lime wedges, to garnish
mixed green salad, to serve

1. Place the turkey breast on a piece of foil large enough to fold
into a sealed parcel. Sprinkle on the shallot or onion and garlic.
2. In a small bowl, mix together the honey, vegetable oil, lime zest
and juice, ground ginger and oregano. Season with salt and pepper.
Spread this over the turkey, turning the breast over to coat it
thoroughly.
3. Fold up and crimp the foil and refrigerate for at least 2 hours,
preferably longer.
4. Cook the potatoes in lightly salted boiling water for 15–20
minutes, or until tender. Drain and keep warm.
5. Meanwhile, preheat the grill to high. Place the sealed turkey
parcel on the rack and cook for 10 minutes. Then open up the foil,
turn the turkey breast, baste and cook for 5 minutes more, or until
it is golden brown.
6. Eat hot or cold, garnished with lime wedges and accompanied
with the boiled potatoes and a mixed green salad.

Cook's note:
If you are out all day this recipe can be prepared in minutes in
the morning and then marinated in the refrigerator until later
in the day.

Selections per serving:
2 Carbohydrate; 1 Fat; 2 Protein; 40 Optional Calories

Selections remaining per day:
2–4 Carbohydrate; 1–2 Fat; 2–3 Fruit; 2 Milk; 1–4 Protein;
3 Vegetable

Variation:
Replace the turkey with lean pork fillet or chicken.

Salmon and Broccoli Bake

Serves 2

Preparation time: 15 minutes
Cooking time: 20 minutes
Calories per serving: 560

Freezing recommended

**If you have some time, make
up a batch of these tasty bakes
for the freezer. They can be
frozen in individual containers
and reheated in the microwave.**

6 oz (180 g) broccoli florets
2 teaspoons margarine
¼ pint (150 ml) skimmed milk
1 tablespoon cornflour

½ teaspoon Dijon mustard
6 oz (180 g) canned salmon,
   drained
1 oz (30 g) button mushrooms,
   sliced thinly
1 teaspoon chopped fresh herbs
   (e.g., chives, parsley and dill)
a pinch of grated nutmeg
3 tablespoons skimmed milk
1 lb (480 g) cooked mashed
   potato
1 teaspoon grated parmesan
   cheese
salt and freshly ground black
   pepper

1. Preheat the oven to Gas Mark 5/190°C/375°F. Cook the broccoli
in lightly salted boiling water for 5–6 minutes or until just tender.
Drain, reserving ¼ pint (150 ml) of the cooking liquor.
2. Melt the margarine in a medium–size saucepan. Remove from
the heat and stir in the milk and cornflour. Cook over a moderate
heat, stirring constantly until the sauce boils and thickens. Reduce
the heat. Stir in the reserved cooking liquor and the mustard. Fold
in the cooked broccoli, salmon, mushrooms and chopped herbs.
Season with salt, pepper and a pinch of grated nutmeg.
3. Spoon the sauce into an ovenproof gratin dish. Mix the milk into
the cooked mashed potato. Spoon the potato on top of the fish and
roughen up the surface with a fork.
4. Sprinkle on the parmesan and bake in the oven for 15–20
minutes, or until the potato topping is golden. Serve at once.

Selections per serving:
2 Carbohydrate; 1 Fat; ¼ Milk; 3 Protein; 1 Vegetable;
30 Optional Calories

Selections remaining per day:
2–4 Carbohydrate; 1–2 Fat; 2–3 Fruit; 1¾ Milk; 0–3 Protein;
2 Vegetable

Variation:
Replace the mushrooms with 3 oz (90 g) sweetcorn kernels.
This will add 40 Optional Calories per serving.

Minced Beef Crumble

Serves 1

Preparation time: 20 minutes
Cooking time: 20 minutes
Calories per serving: 605

Freezing recommended

A tasty savoury crumble
makes a nice topping for this
minced beef meal.

4 oz (120 g) extra–lean minced
  beef
1 shallot or small onion, diced
1 carrot, diced
1 oz (30 g) mushrooms,
  chopped

1 teaspoon plain flour
1/4 pint (150 ml) beef stock
a dash of Worcestershire sauce
salt and freshly ground black
  pepper
For the crumble:
1 oz (30 g) plain flour
1/2 oz (15 g) porridge oats
1/2 teaspoon dried mixed herbs
a pinch of salt
1 teaspoon margarine
1/2 oz (15 g) mature Cheddar
  cheese, grated
To serve:
3 oz (90 g) sweetcorn
2 oz (60 g) peas

1. Gently cook the minced beef and shallot or onion in a small,
non-stick saucepan for 5 minutes, stirring frequently. Add the
carrot and mushrooms and cook for 5 minutes more, stirring well.
Stir in the flour and cook for 1 minute more.
2. Blend in the beef stock and season with a dash of Worcestershire
sauce, salt and pepper. Cover and simmer gently for 10 minutes.
Transfer to a small ovenproof dish.
3. Preheat the oven to Gas Mark 6/190°C/375°F.
4. To make the crumble topping, mix the flour, porridge oats,
mixed herbs and a pinch of salt together in a small bowl. Rub in
the margarine until the mixture resembles breadcrumbs. Mix in
the cheese.
5. Scatter the crumble topping over the meat. Bake for 20 minutes
until golden brown. Meanwhile, cook the sweetcorn and peas in
a small amount of lightly salted boiling water. Serve at once.

Selections per serving:
3 Carbohydrate; 1 Fat; 3 Protein; 1 Vegetable; 40 Optional Calories

Selections remaining per day:
1–3 Carbohydrate; 1–2 Fat; 2–3 Fruit; 2 Milk; 0–3 Protein;
2 Vegetable

Lamb Burgers with a Minty Relish

Serves 2

Preparation and cooking time:
20 minutes
Calories per serving: 465

Freezing not recommended

These burgers are ideal for
serving at summer barbecues.

For the relish:
2 tablespoons finely chopped
  mint
2 spring onions, chopped finely
5 fl oz (150 ml) low-fat natural
  yogurt
2 teaspoons white wine vinegar
artificial sweetener, to taste

For the burgers:
4 teaspoons tomato ketchup
2 teaspoons olive oil
1/2 teaspoon Dijon mustard
1/2 teaspoon dried rosemary
a dash of Worcestershire sauce
1 shallot, chopped finely
8 oz (240 g) lean minced lamb
2 × 2 oz (60 g) pitta breads
1 small Iceberg lettuce,
  shredded
2 tomatoes, sliced
salt and freshly ground black
  pepper

1. Make the relish by mixing all the ingredients together. Sweeten
to taste with a drop of artificial sweetener and season with salt
and pepper. Cover and chill until required.
2. Mix together the tomato ketchup, olive oil, mustard, rosemary
and Worcestershire sauce in a large bowl. Add the shallot and lamb
and mix well. Shape the mixture into 4 patties.
3. Preheat the grill and line the rack with a piece of foil. Grill the
burgers for about 4 minutes on each side until golden brown and
cooked through. Wrap the cooked patties in the foil to keep warm.
4. Toast the pitta breads, cut each one in half and fill each half with
lettuce, sliced tomato, and a pattie. Spoon in a dollop of the minty
relish and serve at once.

Selections per serving:
2 Carbohydrate; 1 Fat; 1/2 Milk; 2 Protein; 1 Vegetable;
70 Optional Calories

Selections remaining per day:
2–4 Carbohydrate; 1–2 Fat; 2–3 Fruit; 11/2 Milk; 1–4 Protein;
2 Vegetable

Vegetable Chilli with Rice

Serves 1

Preparation time: 10 minutes
Cooking time: 30 minutes
Calories per serving: 450

Freezing recommended

(V)

1 teaspoon vegetable oil
1 shallot or small onion, chopped
1 small celery stick, chopped
1 small carrot, sliced
2 oz (60 g) parsnip, chopped
1/2 teaspoon hot chilli powder
1/4 teaspoon paprika
1/4 teaspoon ground cumin
2 teaspoons tomato purée
7 oz (210 g) canned chopped tomatoes
1 oz (30 g) mushrooms, sliced
6 oz (180 g) canned red kidney beans, drained
1/2 teaspoon dried oregano
1 1/2 oz (45 g) long-grain rice
salt and freshly ground black pepper
artificial sweetener (optional)
To serve:
1 tablespoon low-fat natural yogurt
2 teaspoons chopped fresh parsley

1. Heat the oil in a saucepan and gently sauté the shallot, celery and carrot for 5 minutes. Add the parsnip, chilli powder, paprika and ground cumin and cook for 2 minutes more.
2. Stir in the tomato purée, canned tomatoes, mushrooms, kidney beans and oregano and bring to the boil. Cover and simmer for 15 minutes.
3. Cook the rice in plenty of lightly salted boiling water for 10–12 minutes until tender. Drain and keep warm.
4. Season the chilli with salt and pepper and sweeten, if necessary, with a few drops of artificial sweetener. Spoon the rice on to a warm serving plate and top with the chilli. Swirl the yogurt on top and garnish liberally with chopped parsley. Serve at once.

Selections per serving:
2 Carbohydrate; 1 Fat; 2 Protein; 2 Vegetable; 10 Optional Calories

Selections remaining per day:
2–4 Carbohydrate; 1–2 Fat; 2–3 Fruit; 2 Milk; 1–4 Protein; 1 Vegetable

Variations:
Replace the rice with 4 1/2 oz (135 g) of cooked pasta or 3 warm taco shells.
Substitute 3 oz (90 g) of the red kidney beans with an equal amount of cannellini beans or chick peas.

Macaroni with Tomato and Spinach Sauce

Serves 1

Preparation and cooking time: 25 minutes
Calories per serving: 440

Freezing not recommended

(V) **If using vegetarian cheese**

Popular Italian ingredients make up this speedy meal in just minutes.

1 teaspoon olive oil
1 shallot or small onion, chopped finely
1 small celery stick, chopped finely
7 oz (210 g) canned chopped tomatoes
1 teaspoon tomato purée
1 bay leaf
1/2 teaspoon dried oregano
2 oz (60 g) macaroni
2 oz (60 g) frozen spinach, thawed
a pinch of grated nutmeg
2 oz (60 g) mozzarella cheese, sliced thinly
salt and freshly ground black pepper

1. Heat the oil in a small saucepan, and cook the shallot or onion and celery for 5 minutes until softened. Add the chopped tomatoes, tomato purée, bay leaf and oregano. Season with salt and freshly ground black pepper. Simmer, uncovered, for 10 minutes, stirring occasionally.
2. Meanwhile, cook the pasta in lightly boiling salted water for 8–10 minutes or until just *'al dente'*. Drain.
3. Squeeze any excess water out of the spinach. Stir it into the tomato sauce with the nutmeg, and then mix this into the hot pasta.
4. Spoon the pasta and sauce into a small ovenproof dish and arrange the mozzarella slices on top. Place under a hot grill for 5 minutes until the cheese is bubbling. Serve at once.

Cook's note:
Use shallots instead of small onions in your cooking for a less pungent taste and odour.

Selections per serving:
2 Carbohydrate; 1 Fat; 2 Protein; 3 Vegetable

Selections remaining per day:
2–4 Carbohydrate; 1–2 Fat; 2–3 Fruit; 2 Milk; 1–4 Protein

Greek Lamb and Vegetables

Serves 2

Preparation time: 5 minutes
Cooking time: 40 minutes
Calories per serving: 380

Freezing not recommended

This meal of lamb, potatoes and onions with lemon and Mediterranean herbs is both aromatic and easy to prepare.

6 oz (180 g) lean lamb, cubed
1 lb (480 g) new potatoes, halved
2 courgettes, cut in 1-inch (2.5 cm) slices
1 red onion, peeled and quartered
1 lemon, cut in 8
8 whole garlic cloves
1 teaspoon chopped fresh rosemary
1 teaspoon chopped fresh oregano
2 teaspoons olive oil
salt and freshly ground black pepper
fresh rosemary sprigs, to garnish

1. Preheat the oven to Gas Mark 6/200°C/400°F. Place all the ingredients in one layer in a shallow ovenproof dish. Season well with salt and pepper. Shake the dish to lightly coat the ingredients with the oil.
2. Cover with foil and cook for 20 minutes. Remove the foil and squeeze the lemon wedges over the meat, and then tuck them in among the vegetables. Cook for 15–20 minutes more until the meat and vegetables are roasted golden and tender.
3. Divide the lamb and vegetables between 2 warm plates. Discard the lemon wedges, garnish with rosemary sprigs and serve at once.

Cook's note:
Do not be put off by the number of garlic cloves. They will become mild and sweet tasting when roasted.

Selections per serving:
2 Carbohydrate; 1 Fat; 2 Protein; 1 Vegetable

Selections remaining per day:
2–4 Carbohydrate; 1–2 Fat; 2–3 Fruit; 2 Milk; 1–4 Protein; 2 Vegetable

Variation:
Serve the lamb with a minty relish (page 48). This will add 45 Optional Calories.

Braised Lamb Chops

Serves 2

Preparation time: 10 minutes
Cooking time: 30 minutes
Calories per serving: 665

Freezing not recommended

grated zest and juice of 1 medium-size orange
1 teaspoon flour
4 × 3 oz (90 g) lean lamb chops
2 teaspoons vegetable oil
2 carrots, cut in sticks
1 celery stick, sliced thickly
1 leek, sliced thickly
1 garlic clove, chopped finely
4 fresh rosemary sprigs
¼ pint (150 ml) vegetable stock
2 tablespoons white wine
8 oz (240 g) new potatoes, halved
8 oz (240 g) peas
salt and freshly ground black pepper

1. Mix together half of the orange zest with the flour and season well with salt and pepper. Toss the lamb chops in the flour mixture to coat them lightly.
2. Heat 1 teaspoon of the oil in a non-stick saucepan, add the lamb chops and cook for 4 minutes on either side, to seal and brown the meat. Remove from the pan.
3. Heat the remaining oil and add the carrots, celery, leek and garlic. Cook for 5 minutes, stirring occasionally. Stir in the orange juice, 2 rosemary sprigs, the stock and white wine. Bring to the boil and place the lamb chops on top of the bed of vegetables. Cover the pan and simmer for approximately 25 minutes, or until the lamb is very tender.
4. Meanwhile, cook the potatoes in lightly salted boiling water for 15–20 minutes, or until tender. Put the peas on to cook a few minutes before serving. Drain the potatoes and peas and serve on 2 warm plates with the lamb and vegetables. Garnish each serving with a sprig of fresh rosemary and serve at once.

Selections per serving:
2 Carbohydrate; 1 Fat; 3 Protein; 1 Vegetable; 45 Optional Calories

Selections remaining per day:
2–4 Carbohydrate; 1–2 Fat; 2–3 Fruit; 2 Milk; 0–3 Protein; 2 Vegetable

Variation:
Replace the lamb with 2 × 5 oz (150 g) part–boned skinless chicken breasts.

Chicken with Lemon and Garlic

Serves 1

Preparation and cooking time: 30 minutes

Calories per serving: 480

Freezing recommended

1 small lemon
1 garlic clove, chopped
4 oz (120 g) skinless, boneless chicken breast, cut in pieces
8 oz (240 g) potatoes, sliced thickly
3 oz (90 g) carrots, sliced
1 teaspoon olive oil
1 shallot or small onion, diced
6 tablespoons chicken stock
1 teaspoon cornflour
4 tablespoons low–fat natural yogurt
1 tablespoon dry sherry or white wine
2 teaspoons chopped fresh thyme
salt and freshly ground black pepper
a sprig of fresh thyme, to garnish

1. Grate the zest of half the lemon into a bowl. Add the garlic and season with black pepper. Mix in the chicken pieces, coating them well.
2. Cook the potatoes and carrots together in lightly salted boiling water for 10–15 minutes or until tender.
3. Meanwhile, heat the oil in a non-stick frying pan and cook the shallot or onion and chicken pieces for 5 minutes, stirring occasionally. Add the stock and simmer for 5 minutes more.
4. Blend the cornflour with the yogurt and sherry or wine. Stir this in with the chicken and continue to cook, stirring until the sauce thickens slightly. Cut the lemon in half and squeeze in the juice from the grated half.
5. Season with salt and pepper, stir in the fresh thyme and simmer for 2 minutes more.
6. Drain the cooked vegetables and serve on a warm plate. Spoon the chicken and sauce alongside. Garnish with a slice of lemon and a sprig of fresh thyme and serve at once.

Cook's note:
The carrots and potatoes should be sliced to the same thickness so that they cook evenly.

Selections per serving:
2 Carbohydrate; 1 Fat; 3 Protein; 1 Vegetable; 65 Optional Calories

Selections remaining per day:
2–4 Carbohydrate; 1–2 Fat; 2–3 Fruit; 2 Milk; 0–3 Protein; 2 Vegetable

Herby Chicken Roll with Tomato Sauce and Pasta

Serves 2

Preparation time: 20 minutes
Cooking time: 20 minutes
Calories per serving: 395

Freezing recommended (for sauce only)

2 teaspoons vegetable oil
1 small celery stick, chopped finely
1 shallot or small onion, chopped finely
1 small carrot, chopped finely
1 garlic clove, chopped finely
7 oz (210 g) canned chopped tomatoes
1 teaspoon tomato purée
1 bay leaf
6 oz (180 g) skinless, boneless chicken breast
4 teaspoons fresh chopped herbs (e.g., tarragon, dill, chives and parsley)
4 oz (120 g) pasta shapes
1 tablespoon cream
salt and freshly ground black pepper
fresh herbs (e.g., tarragon), to garnish

1. Heat the oil in a saucepan and sauté the celery, shallot or onion, carrot and garlic for 5 minutes. Stir in the canned tomatoes, tomato purée and bay leaf, cover and simmer for 15 minutes.
2. Make a horizontal cut across the chicken breast, opening it up like a book. Place the chicken between 2 sheets of clingfilm and pound it out thinly with a wooden rolling pin. Remove the top layer of clingfilm. Sprinkle the chicken with the herbs and season with salt and freshly ground black pepper. Roll up to form a sausage and wrap tightly with the clingfilm, twisting the ends securely.
3. Bring a large saucepan with plenty of lightly salted water to the boil. Place the chicken roll in the water and simmer for 10 minutes. Remove with tongs, stir the pasta into the water and place the chicken roll back in the saucepan. Cover and cook for 10 minutes or until the pasta is 'al dente'.
4. Meanwhile, liquidise or sieve the tomato sauce. Stir in the cream and season to taste. Divide between 2 warm plates.
5. Drain and divide the pasta between the plates. Remove the clingfilm and slice the chicken roll in 3/4-inch (2 cm) rounds. Serve on top of the pasta and garnish with fresh herbs.

Selections per serving:
2 Carbohydrate; 1 Fat; 2 Protein; 1 1/2 Vegetable; 25 Optional Calories

Selections remaining per day:
2–4 Carbohydrate; 1–2 Fat; 2–3 Fruit; 2 Milk; 1–4 Protein; 1 1/2 Vegetable

Chicken with Peanut Sauce

Serves 1

Preparation and cooking time:
30 minutes
Calories per serving: 490

Freezing recommended

If you enjoy peanut butter, this is a great recipe for making the taste go further!

7 oz (210 g) canned chopped tomatoes
1 shallot or small onion, chopped
1 small garlic clove, chopped
1/2 teaspoon chilli powder
a pinch of cayenne pepper
2 oz (60 g) skinless, boneless chicken thigh, cut in chunks
3 oz (90 g) sweetcorn
1 tablespoon peanut butter
1 teaspoon fresh chopped oregano
2 oz (60 g) long-grain rice
salt and freshly ground black pepper

1. Place the tomatoes, shallot, garlic, chilli powder and a pinch of cayenne pepper in a medium-size saucepan. Cover and simmer gently for 10 minutes.
2. Bring the sauce to the boil and add in the chicken pieces, stirring constantly for 1 minute. Reduce the heat and stir in the sweetcorn, peanut butter and oregano. Season with salt and pepper. Cover and simmer for 15 minutes.
3. Meanwhile, cook the rice in lightly salted boiling water for 10 minutes or until tender. Drain and spoon on to a warm plate. Serve the chicken and sauce on the bed of rice.

Selections per serving:
3 Carbohydrate; 1 Fat; 2 Protein; 2 Vegetable

Selections remaining per day:
1–3 Carbohydrate; 1–2 Fat; 2–3 Fruit; 2 Milk; 1–4 Protein; 1 Vegetable

Variations:
Omit the sweetcorn and increase the quantity of rice to 3 oz (90 g).
    Add 2 tablespoons of white wine to the tomatoes during Step 3. This will add 25 Optional Calories.

Chicken Tikka with Indian-style Salad

Serves 2

Preparation time: 10 minutes
+ 30 minutes marinating
Calories per serving: 355

Freezing not recommended

This popular dish can be prepared well in advance.

6 oz (180 g) skinless, boneless chicken breast, cut in chunks
salt and freshly ground black pepper
fresh coriander, to garnish
2 × 2 oz (60 g) pitta bread, to serve
For the marinade:
6 tablespoons low-fat natural yogurt
2 teaspoons vegetable oil
2 teaspoons lemon juice
1 teaspoon mild chilli powder
1/2 teaspoon paprika
1/2 teaspoon ground cumin
1 small garlic clove, chopped finely
a pinch of ground ginger
salt
For the salad:
2 tomatoes, chopped
2 spring onions, chopped
1/2 small green pepper, de-seeded and chopped
1 tablespoon chopped fresh coriander
1 teaspoon desiccated coconut

1. Combine all of the marinade ingredients in a bowl. Stir in the chicken, making sure that all the pieces are well coated. Cover and refrigerate for 30 minutes.
2. Mix together the salad ingredients. Cover and chill.
3. Thread the marinated chicken on to 2 skewers and grill or barbecue them for 6–8 minutes, turning frequently and brushing with any excess marinade, until the chicken is cooked through and slightly charred.
4. Garnish with fresh coriander and serve with the salad and pitta bread.

Cook's note:
If you use wooden skewers, remember to soak them first in water for 10 minutes to prevent them from burning.

Selections per serving:
2 Carbohydrate; 1 Fat; 2 Protein; 1 Vegetable; 30 Optional Calories

Selections remaining per day:
2–4 Carbohydrate; 1–2 Fat; 2–3 Fruit; 2 Milk; 1–4 Protein; 2 Vegetable

Pork Steaks with Orange and Ginger Glaze

Serves 2

Preparation and cooking time:
30 minutes
Calories per serving: 325

Freezing not recommended

1 lb (480 g) parsnips, cubed
2 teaspoons clear honey
1 teaspoon brown sugar
2 teaspoons vegetable oil
grated zest and juice of
 ¹/₂ medium-size orange
¹/₂ teaspoon coriander seeds,
 crushed coarsely
¹/₂ teaspoon ground ginger
 or 1 teaspoon grated fresh
 root ginger
2 × 5 oz (150 g) lean pork
 steaks
2 tablespoons low-fat natural
 yogurt
2 teaspoons fresh chopped
 parsley
salt and freshly ground black
 pepper
orange slices, to decorate

1. Cook the parsnips in lightly salted boiling water for 15 minutes until soft.
2. Preheat the grill. Mix together the honey, sugar, vegetable oil, orange zest and juice, coriander seeds and ginger in a small bowl. Season well. Brush this on the steaks and cook them under the grill for 15–20 minutes, turning them occasionally and brushing frequently with the marinade.
3. Drain and mash the parsnips with the natural yogurt and chopped parsley. Season to taste.
4. Serve the steaks garnished with fresh orange slices and accompanied by the mashed parsnip.

Cook's note:
Some freshly cooked green vegetables will go well with this meal.

Selections per serving:
2 Carbohydrate; 1 Fat; 3 Protein; 60 Optional Calories

Selections remaining per day:
2–4 Carbohydrate; 1–2 Fat; 2–3 Fruit; 2 Milk; 0–3 Protein;
3 Vegetable

Pork Casserole

Serves 1

Preparation and cooking time:
35 minutes
Calories per serving: 535

Freezing not recommended

**Cooked pears add a subtle
fruitiness to this pork
casserole.**

1 teaspoon vegetable oil
1 onion, sliced
8 oz (240 g) potato, sliced
4 oz (120 g) pork fillet, cut
 into ¹/₂-inch (1 cm) slices
¹/₂ pint (300 ml) chicken or
 vegetable stock
2 teaspoons chopped fresh sage
1 medium-size dessert pear,
 cut in 8
3 oz (90 g) fresh green beans
1 teaspoon cornflour
2 tablespoons low-fat natural
 yogurt
salt and freshly ground black
 pepper
fresh sage leaves, to garnish

1. Heat the oil in a small flameproof casserole. Cook the onion gently for 8–10 minutes until softened and golden. Add the potato and cook for 5 minutes more. Remove the vegetables from the pan and set aside.
2. Add the pork to the hot pan and cook briskly for 2 minutes on each side, to seal and brown the meat. Return the onion and potato to the pan and add the stock and sage. Bring to the boil, and then reduce the heat and simmer, uncovered, for 15 minutes. Add the pear and simmer for 10 minutes more.
3. Meanwhile, cook the beans in lightly salted boiling water for 6 minutes, or until just tender.
4. Blend the cornflour into the yogurt and stir it in with the pork casserole. Simmer for 3–4 minutes, stirring occasionally until the sauce thickens slightly. Season with salt and pepper to taste.
5. Drain the beans and serve them with the casserole, garnished with sage leaves.

Selections per serving:
2 Carbohydrate; 1 Fat; 1 Fruit; 3 Protein; 1¹/₂ Vegetable;
30 Optional Calories

Selections remaining per day:
2–4 Carbohydrate; 1–2 Fat; 1–2 Fruit; 2 Milk; 0–3 Protein;
1¹/₂ Vegetable

Beef in a Peppercorn Sauce

Serves 1

Preparation and cooking time:
25 minutes
Calories per serving: 345

Freezing not recommended

**Treat yourself to tender fillet
of beef cooked with a delicate
red wine and peppercorn
sauce.**

4 oz (120 g) new potatoes,
 scrubbed

1 teaspoon vegetable oil
3 oz (90 g) beef fillet
1 shallot or small onion,
 chopped finely
2 teaspoons green peppercorns
2 tablespoons red wine
4 oz (120 g) peas
6 tablespoons beef stock
1 teaspoon coarse-grained
 mustard
chopped parsley, to garnish
salt and freshly ground black
 pepper

1. Cook the potatoes in lightly salted boiling water for 15 minutes until tender. Drain and keep warm.
2. Meanwhile, heat the oil in a small non-stick frying pan. Cook the beef for 2 minutes on each side, to seal in the juices. Transfer to a plate.
3. Add the shallot or onion and peppercorns and cook gently for 4–5 minutes until the shallot turns golden. Add the red wine and cook for 3–4 minutes, or until the wine has reduced by half.
4. Meanwhile, cook the peas in lightly salted boiling water, drain and keep warm.
5. Return the beef to the pan. Add the stock, increase the heat and cook rapidly for 3–4 minutes to reduce and thicken the sauce and cook the steak through. (The sauce will become syrupy.)
6. Transfer the beef to a warm serving plate. Stir the mustard into the sauce, season with salt and pepper and pour over the steak. Garnish with freshly chopped parsley and serve with the potatoes and peas.

Cook's note:
You can now buy excellent-quality fresh stocks. For small quantities, freeze the stock in ice-cube containers and store in plastic bags until needed.

Selections per serving:
2 Carbohydrate; 1 Fat; 2 Protein; ½ Vegetable;
25 Optional Calories

Selections remaining per day:
2–4 Carbohydrate; 1–2 Fat; 2–3 Fruit; 2 Milk; 1–4 Protein;
2½ Vegetable

Beef and Ginger Stir-Fry with Noodles

Serves 1

Preparation time: 10 minutes
+ 20 minutes marinating
Cooking time: 10 minutes
Calories per serving: 480

Freezing not recommended

**Stir-fries are a great way of
cooking food – fast, tasty and
with hardly any washing up.**

1 teaspoon dry sherry
2 teaspoons sherry vinegar
2 teaspoons light soy sauce
1 small garlic clove, chopped
 finely

1 teaspoon finely grated fresh
 root ginger or ½ teaspoon
 ground ginger
3 oz (90 g) fillet steak, cut in
 strips
1 teaspoon vegetable oil
2 oz (60 g) noodles
2 spring onions, chopped in
 2-inch (5 cm) lengths
¼ red pepper, de-seeded and
 cut in strips
½ teaspoon dried crushed
 chillies
½ teaspoon sesame seeds
2 oz (60 g) broccoli florets
2 oz (60 g) fresh spinach or
 Chinese leaf, shredded

1. Mix together the sherry, vinegar, soy sauce, garlic and ginger in a shallow dish. Stir in the beef and leave to marinate for 20 minutes.
2. Put a saucepan of lightly salted water on to boil. Heat the oil in a frying pan or wok until very hot.
3. Add the strips of beef to the frying pan, reserving any extra marinade. Stir-fry for 2 minutes. Cook the noodles in the boiling water for 5 minutes and then drain and keep warm.
4. Add the spring onions, red pepper, dried chillies, sesame seeds, broccoli florets and spinach or Chinese leaf to the wok. Stir-fry for 3 minutes. Pour in any reserved marinade and stir-fry for 1 minute more.
5. Arrange the noodles on a serving plate. Top with the stir-fry and serve at once.

Selections per serving:
2 Carbohydrate; 1 Fat; 2 Protein; 1 Vegetable; 10 Optional Calories

Selections remaining per day:
2–4 Carbohydrate; 1–2 Fat; 2–3 Fruit; 2 Milk; 1–4 Protein;
2 Vegetable

Seafood Stir-Fry

Serves 1

Preparation and cooking time:
10 minutes
Calories per serving: 325

Freezing not recommended

This has to be the speediest
supper dish – just what you
need after a busy day at work.

1 teaspoon vegetable oil
1 Little Gem lettuce, shredded
1 small celery stick, cut in
  matchsticks
1 small carrot, cut in
  matchsticks
5 oz (150 g) mixed seafood
  (e.g., haddock or cod, cooked
  squid rings, and cooked
  mussels or peeled prawns)
1 garlic clove, chopped
2 oz (60 g) whole baby
  sweetcorn
juice of ½ lemon
1 teaspoon chopped fresh herbs
  (e.g., chives, dill and parsley)
salt and freshly ground black
  pepper
1 lemon wedge, to garnish
6 oz (180 g) cooked noodles,
  to serve

1. Heat the oil in a non-stick frying pan or wok. Add the lettuce
and stir-fry for 30 seconds or until lightly cooked. Transfer to
a serving plate and keep warm.
2. Stir-fry the celery, carrot, haddock or cod, garlic and baby
sweetcorn. Add the lemon juice and stir-fry for 2 minutes.
3. Stir in the squid rings and mussels or prawns. Toss together well,
adding the herbs, some salt and plenty of ground black pepper.
4. Spoon the stir-fry over the shredded lettuce, garnish with a
wedge of lemon and serve at once with the cooked noodles.

Cook's note:
If you buy your fish from the supermarket's fish counter it is easier
to get a selection of small quantities of fish – ideal for this recipe.

Selections per serving:
2 Carbohydrate; 1 Fat; 2 Protein; 2 Vegetable; 40 Optional Calories

Selections remaining per day:
2–4 Carbohydrate; 1–2 Fat; 2–3 Fruit; 2 Milk; 1–4 Protein;
1 Vegetable

Seafood in a Creamy Tomato Sauce

Serves 1

Preparation and cooking time:
25 minutes
Calories per serving: 505

Freezing recommended

Canned tomatoes have to be
a firm favourite of Weight
Watchers cooks. They are
handy, economical and make
so many tasty dishes.

1 teaspoon olive oil
1 small onion, sliced
2 oz (60 g) button mushrooms,
  sliced
7 oz (210 g) canned chopped
  tomatoes
2 oz (60 g) long-grain rice
1 tablespoon white wine
4 oz (120 g) firm white fish
  (e.g., haddock), cubed
2 oz (60 g) cooked peeled
  prawns
1 tablespoon chopped fresh
  coriander or basil
2 tablespoons natural fromage
  frais (up to 8% fat)
salt and freshly ground black
  pepper

1. Heat the olive oil in a medium-size saucepan and gently cook
the onion for 4–5 minutes, until softened. Add the mushrooms
and tomatoes. Bring to the boil, and then cover and simmer for
5 minutes.
2. Meanwhile, cook the rice in lightly salted boiling water
according to the pack instructions. Drain and keep warm.
3. Stir the wine, fish and prawns into the tomato sauce. Add half
of the chopped herbs and cook gently for 3–4 minutes until the
fish is opaque and flakes easily. Season to taste.
4. Spoon the rice on to a warm serving plate. Using a slotted
spoon, transfer the fish on to the bed of rice. Stir the fromage frais
into the tomato sauce and pour this over the fish. Sprinkle with
the remaining chopped herbs and serve at once.

Cook's note:
Cooked rice freezes very successfully and can be reheated in the
microwave or in a saucepan with a couple of tablespoons of water.
Weigh out 3 oz (90 g) portions and seal in freezer bags.

Selections per serving:
2 Carbohydrate; 1 Fat; 2 Protein; 3 Vegetable; 60 Optional Calories

Selections remaining per day:
2–4 Carbohydrate; 1–2 Fat; 2–3 Fruit; 2 Milk; 1–4 Protein

Salmon and Asparagus Risotto

Serves 1

Preparation and cooking time:
30 minutes
Calories per serving: 495

Freezing not recommended

Sometimes cooking for one seems to be more trouble than it's worth. This recipe is so quick and easy that you'll want to eat solo more often!

2 oz (60 g) mixed wild and
    long-grain rice
7 fl oz (210 ml) vegetable stock

3 oz (90 g) salmon fillet, cubed
1 teaspoon lemon juice
1 teaspoon chopped fresh dill
3 oz (90 g) fresh asparagus, cut
    in 2-inch (5 cm) lengths
1 small tomato, diced
1 teaspoon olive oil
1 tablespoon single cream or
    crème fraîche
salt and freshly ground black
    pepper
a sprig of fresh dill, to garnish

1. Place the rice and stock in a medium-size saucepan and slowly bring to the boil. Meanwhile, lay the salmon fillet on a piece of greaseproof paper. Sprinkle with the lemon juice and chopped dill, season with salt and pepper, and then fold the greaseproof paper to form a parcel.
2. Carefully place the salmon parcel in the saucepan on top of the rice. Add the asparagus, cover and reduce the heat and let simmer for 8–10 minutes, or until nearly all the stock has been absorbed and the rice is tender.
3. Unwrap the salmon parcel and tip the fish back with the rice. Gently flake it with a fork. Stir in the diced tomato, the olive oil and cream or crème fraîche. Fold together all the ingredients and season to taste.
4. Serve the risotto on a warm plate, garnished with a sprig of fresh dill.

Cook's note:
Try chilling the risotto – it tastes equally delicious when eaten cold.

Selections per serving:
2 Carbohydrate; 1 Fat; 2 Protein; 1 Vegetable; 50 Optional Calories

Selections remaining per day:
2–4 Carbohydrate; 1–2 Fat; 2–3 Fruit; 2 Milk; 1–4 Protein;
2 Vegetable

Tuna Fishcakes with Sweetcorn Relish

Serves 1

Preparation time: 15 minutes
Cooking time: 20 minutes
Calories per serving: 475

Freezing recommended
(at the end of step 2)

These tasty fishcakes make the most of canned tuna fish.

2 oz (60 g) canned tuna in
    brine, drained
4 oz (120 g) cooked mashed
    potato
1 teaspoon margarine
2 teaspoons tomato purée
2 teaspoons fresh snipped
    chives
1 teaspoon lemon juice

1 egg, beaten
2 tablespoons dried
    breadcrumbs
4 oz (120 g) green beans
salt and freshly ground black
    pepper
For the sweetcorn relish:
1 oz (30 g) canned sweetcorn
    kernels
1 spring onion, chopped finely
2 teaspoons tomato purée
1/2 teaspoon clear honey
1 teaspoon capers or 1 gherkin,
    chopped finely
salt and freshly ground black
    pepper
To garnish:
fresh parsley
lemon wedge

1. Preheat the oven to Gas Mark 5/190°C/375°F. Mix the tuna, mashed potato, margarine, tomato purée, chives and lemon juice in a bowl. Season well and mix in 1 tablespoon of the beaten egg.
2. Place the remaining beaten egg in a saucer with 1 tablespoon of water. Place the breadcrumbs in a shallow bowl.
3. Form the fish and potato mixture into 2 fishcakes. Dip the fishcakes in the egg and then coat them with the breadcrumbs.
4. Place the fishcakes on a non-stick baking tray and cook for 15–20 minutes or until golden brown.
5. Meanwhile, make the relish. Mix together the sweetcorn kernels, spring onion, tomato purée, honey and capers or chopped gherkin. Season with salt and pepper to taste.
6. Cook the green beans in lightly salted boiling water for 6 minutes or until just tender. Drain.
7. Serve the fishcakes with the relish and the green beans. Garnish with a sprig of parsley and a lemon wedge.

Selections per serving:
2 Carbohydrate; 1 Fat; 2 Protein; 1 Vegetable; 35 Optional Calories

Selections remaining per day:
2–4 Carbohydrate; 1–2 Fat; 2–3 Fruit; 2 Milk; 1–4 Protein;
2 Vegetable

Oriental Cod Steaks

Serves 1

Preparation and cooking time:
25 minutes
Calories per serving: 425

Freezing not recommended

This is one parcel you will
enjoy opening – cod is
delicious with roasted baby
sweetcorn.

3 oz (90 g) baby sweetcorn
1 teaspoon sesame or olive oil
1/2 teaspoon sesame seeds
6 oz (180 g) cod steak
2 teaspoons lemon juice
1 spring onion, shredded
1/2 small courgette
1/2 carrot
1/2 teaspoon finely chopped
    fresh ginger
2 teaspoons light soy sauce
1 oz (30 g) long-grain rice

1. Preheat the oven to Gas Mark 7/210°C/425°F.
2. Cook the baby sweetcorn in lightly salted boiling water for
3 minutes. Drain and refresh under cold running water. Drain
again. Toss in the oil and sesame seeds and place in a shallow
ovenproof dish.
3. Lay the cod steak on a piece of foil. Drizzle with the lemon juice
and scatter with the spring onion. Using a potato peeler, pare
ribbons of courgette and carrot over the fish. Sprinkle on the ginger
and soy sauce. Wrap the fish up to form a sealed parcel and place
it on a baking sheet with the baby sweetcorn alongside. Cook for
12–15 minutes.
4. Meanwhile, cook the rice in lightly salted boiling water according
to the pack instructions. Drain and keep warm.
5. Spoon the roasted baby sweetcorns on to a warm plate. Carefully
open the parcel and slide the fish and vegetables on to the plate.
Serve at once with the rice.

Selections per serving:
2 Carbohydrate; 1 Fat; 2 Protein; 1 Vegetable; 5 Optional Calories

Selections remaining per day:
2–4 Carbohydrate; 1–2 Fat; 2–3 Fruit; 2 Milk; 1–4 Protein;
2 Vegetable

Roasted Trout and Vegetables

Serves 2

Preparation time: 10 minutes
Cooking time: 60 minutes
Calories per serving: 385

Freezing not recommended

An excellent method of cooking
a complete meal – the fish
bakes on a bed of vegetables.

2 × 8 oz (240 g) baking potatoes
1 small fennel bulb (optional)
2 × 5 oz (150 g) trout, cleaned

2 teaspoons olive oil
6 oz (180 g) carrots, cut in
    sticks
1 courgette, cut in sticks
1 lemon
4 tablespoons white wine
4 tablespoons low-fat natural
    yogurt
1 teaspoon chopped fresh dill
salt and freshly ground black
    pepper
fresh dill, to garnish

1. Preheat the oven to Gas Mark 6/200°C/400°F. Prick the potatoes
with a fork and sprinkle with salt. Place on a baking tray and bake
for 60 minutes. Half–way through the baking time continue
preparing the rest of the meal.
2. Cut the fennel in quarters (if using), trim any tough stalk
and cut the bulb in thin slices.
3. Spread the fennel in a shallow ovenproof dish large enough to
hold the trout. Drizzle the oil over and bake for 10 minutes, and
then stir in the carrots and courgette. Place the trout on top. Cut
the lemon in half and squeeze the juice of one half over the fish
and vegetables (cut the other half in wedges and reserve). Pour
the wine over and season well with salt and pepper. Cook for
20 minutes, or until the trout is tender.
4. Using a fish slice, transfer the trout and vegetables on to 2 warm
plates. Stir the yogurt and dill into the remaining cooking juices.
Season and then spoon the sauce over the vegetables. Garnish with
the reserved lemon wedges and fresh dill. Serve at once with the
baked potato.

Selections per serving:
2 Carbohydrate; 1 Fat; 3 Protein; 2 Vegetable; 45 Optional Calories

Selections remaining per day:
2–4 Carbohydrate; 1–2 Fat; 2–3 Fruit; 2 Milk; 0–3 Protein;
1 Vegetable

Variation:
This method works well with fish steaks too: reduce the cooking
time for the fish to 15 minutes.

Cod with Mustard Sauce

Serves 1

Preparation and cooking time:
20 minutes
Calories per serving: 420

Freezing not recommended

White fish and mustard may
seem unusual at first, but it
is a delicious combination.

4 oz (120 g) potatoes
2 teaspoons low-fat spread
1 shallot or small onion,
  chopped finely

4 oz (120 g) peas
3 oz (90 g) carrots, chopped
6 oz (180 g) fresh cod fillet or
  steak, skinned
5 fl oz (150 ml) skimmed milk
1 tablespoon plain flour
1–2 teaspoons Dijon mustard
2 teaspoons chopped fresh
  parsley
salt and freshly ground black
  pepper
fresh parsley, to garnish

1. Cook the potatoes in lightly salted boiling water for 15–20 minutes, or until tender. Drain and keep warm.
2. Melt the low-fat spread in a small saucepan and cook the shallot or onion gently for 5 minutes until softened but not coloured.
3. Cook the peas and carrots in lightly salted boiling water for 5–8 minutes, or until just tender. Drain and keep warm.
4. Lay the fish in a small frying pan, pour the milk over it, cover and slowly bring to the boil. Reduce the heat and simmer for 5 minutes or until the fish flakes easily. Carefully transfer the fish to a plate and keep warm, reserving the milk.
5. Stir the flour in with the shallot or onion and cook for 2 minutes. Gradually blend in the hot milk from the frying pan. Bring back to the boil, stirring constantly until the sauce has thickened and is smooth. Stir in the mustard and parsley. Season with salt and pepper.
6. Pour the mustard sauce over the fish. Garnish with a sprig of fresh parsley and serve with the potatoes, carrots and peas.

Selections per serving:
2 Carbohydrate; 1 Fat; 1/2 Milk; 2 Protein; 2 Vegetable;
30 Optional Calories

Selections remaining per day:
2–4 Carbohydrate; 1–2 Fat; 2–3 Fruit; 1 1/2 Milk; 1–4 Protein;
1 Vegetable

Variation:
Experiment with different mustards – coarse-grained or tarragon-flavoured mustards are both tasty options.

Desserts

Desserts are often regarded as pure indulgence, and in many slimming programmes they are strictly forbidden. But Weight Watchers know that these treats will keep you 'sweet' and on track with the rest of the Programme. So you can stay slim and trim with these delicious desserts and puddings. ≈≈ Use these recipes as 'add-ons' to your Selections for your Main Meal, making full use of your daily Selections allowance.

Peach Mousse

Serves 2

Preparation time: 15 minutes
+ 30 minutes chilling
Calories per serving: 125

Freezing not recommended

V If using a free-range egg

You can whip up this light and refreshing mousse using your favourite soft fruits.

7 oz (210 g) canned peaches
  in natural juice, drained with
  2 tablespoons of juice reserved
1 teaspoon powdered gelatine
5 fl oz (150 ml) low-fat natural
  yogurt
2 tablespoons single cream
a few drops of artificial
  sweetener
1 egg white
mint leaves, to decorate

1. Place the 2 tablespoons of natural fruit juice in a small bowl. Sprinkle the gelatine on top and place the bowl in a pan of hot water for a few minutes, until the gelatine has dissolved. Cool for 5 minutes.
2. Slice 2 pieces of peach and reserve for decoration. Purée the remainder with the yogurt and cream in a liquidiser or blender until smooth. Sweeten with artificial sweetener to taste. Blend in the cooled gelatine thoroughly.
3. Beat the egg white in a grease-free bowl until it is stiff but not dry. Fold it in with the peach mixture. Pour into 2 glasses and refrigerate until lightly set. Decorate each with a slice of peach and a fresh mint leaf before serving.

Selections per serving:
1/2 Fruit; 1/2 Milk; 80 Optional Calories

Selections remaining per day:
4–6 Carbohydrate; 2–3 Fat; 11/2–21/2 Fruit; 11/2 Milk; 3–6 Protein; 3 Vegetable

Variation:
Serve the mousse with fresh raspberries when available. Allow 2 oz (60 g) per serving and add 1/2 Fruit Selection.

Baked Apple Pudding

Serves 1

Preparation time: 10 minutes
Cooking time: 30 minutes
Calories per serving: 195

Freezing recommended
(at end of step 3)

V

This is a warming pudding on a cold winter's day – and just as delicious eaten chilled.

1 medium-size cooking apple,
  sliced
2 teaspoons sultanas
2 teaspoons ground almonds
2 teaspoons golden syrup
1/4 teaspoon grated orange zest
juice of 1 medium-size orange
a pinch of ground ginger
a pinch of mixed spice
2 tablespoons fromage frais
  (up to 8% fat)

1. Preheat the oven to Gas Mark 6/200°C/400°F. Layer the apple slices, sultanas and ground almonds in a ramekin dish or ovenproof bowl.
2. Mix together the golden syrup, half of the grated orange zest, the orange juice, ginger and mixed spice and pour over the apple.
3. Cover with a piece of foil and bake for 20 minutes, or until the apple is very tender.
4. Mix the remaining orange zest into the fromage frais and serve with the baked apple.

Cook's note:
Replace the apple with 6 oz (180 g) rhubarb which goes well with orange, although you may need to add artificial sweetener. This will reduce your Fruit Selection to 1.

Selections per serving:
2 Fruit; 1/2 Protein; 75 Optional Calories

Selections remaining per day:
4–6 Carbohydrate; 2–3 Fat; 0–1 Fruit; 2 Milk; 21/2–51/2 Protein; 3 Vegetable

Crunchy Banana Whip

Serves 1

Preparation time: 10 minutes
+ 5 minutes chilling
Calories per serving: 195

Freezing not recommended

(V)

1 small banana
2 teaspoons lemon juice
2 teaspoons clear honey
3 fl oz (90 ml) low-fat natural
  yogurt
1 small gingernut biscuit,
  crushed

**Bananas are a great source of
energy and taste great in this
crunchy treat.**

1. Slice the banana and toss it in the lemon juice. Mash or purée
two-thirds of the banana slices with the honey and yogurt.
2. Spoon half of the purée into a small ramekin or glass dish.
Scatter half of the biscuit crumbs over. Cover with the remaining
purée and top with the rest of the biscuit crumbs.
3. Decorate with the reserved banana slices. Chill for 5 minutes
before serving.

Selections per serving:
1 Fruit; ¹/₂ Milk; 90 Optional Calories

Selections remaining per day:
4–6 Carbohydrate; 2–3 Fat; 1–2 Fruit; 1¹/₂ Milk; 3–6 Protein;
3 Vegetable

Rhubarb and Strawberry Meringue

Serves 2

Preparation and cooking time:
15 minutes
Calories per serving: 65

Freezing not recommended

(V) If using a free-range egg

8 oz (240 g) rhubarb, cut in
  1-inch (2.5 cm) pieces
a few drops of artificial
  sweetener
4 oz (120 g) strawberries, sliced
  thinly
1 egg white
1 tablespoon caster sugar

1. Cook the rhubarb gently in a small amount of water for
5 minutes, or until just tender. Add artificial sweetener to taste
and stir in the sliced strawberries.
2. Divide the fruit between 2 ramekin dishes or small flameproof
bowls.
3. Beat the egg white in a grease-free bowl until stiff and whisk
in the sugar a little at a time. Spoon this on top of the fruit.
4. Grill for 3–4 minutes until the meringue is set and lightly
golden. Serve warm.

Selections per serving:
¹/₂ Fruit; 40 Optional Calories

Selections remaining per day:
4–6 Carbohydrate; 2–3 Fat; 1¹/₂–2¹/₂ Fruit; 2 Milk; 3–6 Protein;
3 Vegetable

Variation:
Replace the rhubarb with 8 oz (240 g) gooseberries, simmering
them until very tender. This will add 1 Fruit Selection – remember
to deduct these from your remaining Selections.

...nd Banana Pudding

...e: 15 minutes
...ooling
... 15 minutes
...serving: 150

...ot recommended

...ng a free-range egg

...y real comfort food –
...my hot pudding to
...fy the sweetest tooth!

7 fl oz (210 ml) skimmed milk
1/2 oz (15 g) ground rice
2 teaspoons cocoa powder
1 egg, separated
2 teaspoons caster sugar
1 small banana, sliced
1/2 teaspoon icing sugar, sieved

...Preheat the oven to Gas Mark 5/190°C/375°F.
...Put the milk, ground rice and cocoa powder in a small saucepan
...and heat gently, stirring constantly with a wooden spoon until it
comes to the boil. Simmer for 5 minutes, stirring frequently.
Remove from the heat and allow to cool for 15 minutes.
3. In a grease-free bowl, whisk the egg white until it is stiff. Beat
the egg yolk and caster sugar into the rice mixture. Gently fold
in the egg white.
4. Divide the banana between 2 individual ovenproof dishes
or ramekins. Spoon the rice mixture evenly over top. Bake for
15 minutes until risen and lightly set. Dust with icing sugar
and serve at once.

Cook's note:
Rice flour can be used instead of ground rice. If you like the
combination of nutmeg or cinnamon with chocolate, sprinkle
a pinch over the bananas before baking.

Selections per serving:
1/2 Fruit; 1/4 Milk; 1/2 Protein; 60 Optional Calories

Selections remaining per day:
4–6 Carbohydrate; 2–3 Fat; 11/2–21/2 Fruit; 13/4 Milk;
21/2–51/2 Protein; 3 Vegetable

Tipsy Chocolate Fondue

Serves 1

Preparation and cooking time:
15 minutes
Calories per serving: 380

Freezing not recommended

Ⓥ

**Deliciously indulgent – chunks
of fruit dunked into a warm
and creamy chocolate fondue!**

1/4 pint (150 ml) skimmed milk
1 teaspoon cornflour

1 teaspoon cocoa powder
1/2 small banana, cut in chunks
1/2 kiwi fruit, peeled and cut
  in thick slices
1 oz (30 g) fresh or canned
  pineapple, cut in chunks
1/2 medium-size orange,
  segmented
3 ratafia biscuits
1 teaspoon rum, brandy or
  Cointreau
artificial sweetener, to taste
a drop of vanilla essence

1. Blend a tablespoon of the milk with the cornflour and cocoa
powder to make a smooth paste. Put the remaining milk in a small
saucepan and bring slowly to the boil.
2. Place a small bowl in the centre of a serving plate. Arrange the
prepared fruit and ratafia biscuits around it.
3. Whisk the cornflour and cocoa paste into the boiling milk,
stirring constantly until the sauce has thickened and is smooth.
Remove from the heat and stir in the rum, brandy or Cointreau.
Sweeten to taste with a little artificial sweetener and stir in a drop
of vanilla essence. Pour into the serving bowl and serve at once.

Selections per serving:
11/2 Fruit; 1/2 Milk; 225 Optional Calories

Selections remaining per day:
4–6 Carbohydrate; 2–3 Fat; 1/2–11/2 Fruit; 11/2 Milk; 3–6 Protein;
3 Vegetable

Variation:
For a really speedy fondue, gently melt 2 oz (60 g) of chocolate ice-
cream, stir in the rum, brandy or Cointreau and serve at once.
This will increase your Optional Calories to 300 in addition to
your Fruit and Milk Selections.

Raspberry Brulée

Serves 2

Preparation and cooking time:
35 minutes
Calories per serving: 195

Freezing not recommended

Ⓥ

1 oz (30 g) short-grain or
   pudding rice
½ pint (300 ml) skimmed milk
2 tablespoons single cream
a drop of vanilla essence
artificial sweetener, to taste
4 oz (120 g) fresh raspberries
4 teaspoons demerara sugar

This warm and creamy
raspberry rice pudding has a
delicious caramelised topping.

1. Place the rice and milk in a small saucepan. Bring to the boil
and then reduce the heat and simmer very gently for about 25
minutes, stirring frequently, until the rice is cooked and most of
the milk has been absorbed.
2. Stir in the cream and add a few drops of vanilla essence and
artificial sweetener to taste. Preheat the grill.
3. Fold in the raspberries and divide between 2 individual
flameproof ramekin dishes. Sprinkle with the demerara sugar.
4. Place under a hot grill for approximately 1 minute or until the
sugar has caramelised. Serve at once.

Selections per serving:
½ Carbohydrate; ½ Fruit; ½ Milk; 90 Optional Calories

Selections remaining per day:
3½–5½ Carbohydrate; 2–3 Fat; 1½–2½ Fruit; 1½ Milk;
3–6 Protein; 3 Vegetable

Variation:
Replace the raspberries with 4 oz (120 g) apricots or peaches.
You can use fresh fruit or canned in natural juices, with the
juices drained.

Pear Sundae with Chocolate Sauce

Serves 2

Preparation and cooking time:
10 minutes + 15 minutes
cooling
Calories per serving: 265

Freezing not recommended

Ⓥ

4 teaspoons cocoa powder
4 teaspoons golden syrup
2 teaspoons margarine
8 oz (240 g) canned pear halves
   in natural juice, drained with
   2 tablespoons juice reserved
4 oz (120 g) vanilla ice-cream
1 teaspoon toasted chopped
   hazelnuts

This is an old favourite
of mine that still goes
down well!

1. Combine the cocoa powder, golden syrup and margarine in
a small saucepan and heat gently, stirring constantly. Add the
2 tablespoons of reserved juice and simmer for a couple of minutes.
Leave to cool for 15 minutes.
2. Divide the pear halves between 2 individual glass dishes, spoon
the ice-cream on top and then top with the chocolate sauce.
Sprinkle with the hazelnuts and serve at once.

Cook's note:
This chocolate sauce can be kept refrigerated for several days and
reheated slowly. It is best served just barely warm.

Selections per serving:
1 Fat; 1 Fruit; 165 Optional Calories

Selections remaining per day:
4–6 Carbohydrate; 1–2 Fat; 1–2 Fruit; 2 Milk; 3–6 Protein;
3 Vegetable

Creamy Honey Syllabub

Serves 2

Preparation time: 10 minutes
+ 10 minutes chilling
Calories per serving: 195

Freezing not recommended

Ⓥ **If using a free-range egg**

Try one of the more exotic
and stronger flavoured honeys
available – orange blossom,
lavender or heather. They each
have a unique flavour which
will taste delicious in this
creamy syllabub.

4 teaspoons clear honey
4 teaspoons sherry
5 oz (150 g) fromage frais
(up to 8% fat)
1 egg white
2 teaspoons icing sugar, sieved
1/2 oz (15 g) toasted flaked
almonds, to decorate

1. Whisk together the honey, sherry and fromage frais.
2. In a grease-free bowl, whisk the egg white until stiff. Fold
the icing sugar in with it.
3. Carefully fold the sweetened egg white in with the fromage
frais mixture. Spoon into 2 individual glass dishes and chill for
10 minutes.
4. Scatter the toasted almonds on top of each portion just
before serving.

Cook's note:
Syllabub has a tendency to separate, so it needs to be eaten
without too much delay.

Selections per serving:
1/2 Fat; 1 Protein; 110 Optional Calories

Selections remaining per day:
4–6 Carbohydrate; 1 1/2–2 1/2 Fat; 2–3 Fruit; 2 Milk; 2–5 Protein;
3 Vegetable

Apricot Velvet

Serves 1

Preparation time: 10 minutes
+ 15 minutes chilling
Calories per serving: 175

Freezing not recommended

Ⓥ

Canned fruits are versatile
and give us variety all the year
round. Be sure to buy fruits
packed in natural juice.

4 oz (120 g) canned apricots
in natural juice, drained
and halved
1 cardamom pod, lightly
crushed to release the seeds
1 teaspoon clear honey
1 teaspoon Cointreau or fruit
brandy
4 fl oz (120 ml) low-fat natural
yogurt
3 ratafia biscuits

1. Reserve 1 apricot half. Blend the remaining apricots, cardamom
seeds, honey and Cointreau or fruit brandy in a liquidiser or food
processor for 20 seconds until smooth.
2. Fold the apricot purée in with the yogurt and pour in a serving
dish. Decorate with the remaining apricot half and cover and chill
for 15 minutes. Serve with the ratafia biscuits.

Selections per serving:
1 Fruit; 1/2 Milk; 280 Optional Calories

Selections remaining per day:
4–6 Carbohydrate; 2–3 Fat; 1–2 Fruit; 1 1/2 Milk; 3–6 Protein;
3 Vegetable

Variation:
Substitute 4 oz (120 g) canned peaches or canned mango for
the apricot. Make sure they are packed in natural juice.

Index